The Marriage-Work Connection

"Dr. Block draws on his extensive expertise and the experiences of real-life couples to put together a comprehensive turnaround plan for the executive marriage. He presents his Power Strategies in a way that busy executives can readily understand and apply, both at home and in business."
—Ann Bevans-Selig, president, Bevans Group

"Holy cow! How refreshing it is to finally see someone break it down for us and make us realize how a strong marriage is key to being successful both personally and professionally. Joel highlights how marriage-strengthening principles have a direct relationship with smart business tactics. Thanks, Joel, for bringing this book to so many people."
—Zee Simmons, CEO/Z Force Consulting Services Group Inc.

"Finally! A book that executives can use to see how their behavior impacts the bottom line in their relationships! While there are a great many other books on relationships out there, Dr. Block's book is the first one I've found that writes about relationships in a way that business leaders will understand. By skillfully writing about the complexities of relationships and framing them in a "business" context, Dr. Block's book is filled with highly useful stories and practical advice that any executive would appreciate if they're looking for a better return on investment from their personal lives.
—Jim Jenkins, president, Creative Visions Consulting

"Dr. Block illustrates the urgency facing executives and their organizations when per-sonal pressures are combined with today's everyday work issues.... If you're looking for a real-life action plan that integrates successful business tactics with strategies for deepening marital love, you won't be disappointed."
—Debra C. Schoenstein, senior partner, S. Hollins Selfridge; LeaderAlliance.com

"As I read through the book I gasped in amazement—I saw myself in so many different scenarios. This book was an eye-opener and a real help in getting a handle on the balance between my personal life and my professional responsibilities."
—Dr. Joan Dellavalle, principal, Otsego Elementary School, Dix Hills, New York

"What works for me is compassion, love, listening, yielding. Dr. Block guides us to each of these life sources in his wonderful book. Being married to a successful executive, I couldn't hope for a better book to provide clear direction. It is filled with the author's warmth and down-to-earth advice."
—Joan Levine, former real estate entrepreneur; SUNY Alumni Award Winner for Excellence in Business

"Anyone in a marriage, who is involved in the corporate world, should consider this book mandatory reading or suffer the consequences Dr. Block so clearly identifies."
—Annie Loring, television commercial producer

"Dr. Block, in his insightful, provocative book, has it precisely right. It's not enough to be able to manage millions, have a business that can't function without you, or be the brawn behind the operation, if you can't get a hug from the one you love."
—Ivy L. Leibowitz, Special Professor of Law, Hofstra University

"Dr. Block is right on. It's all intertwined. Power, respect, love all make for a better executive and a successful marriage."
—Helene Cohen, National Accounts Manager, Fisher-Price

"I've been researching issues working adults identify as major challenges in their careers for over the past decade. The number one issue, without question, is life/work balance. This issue is magnified for executives and their spouses. Dr. Block's ten power strategies are timely, and right on the money."
—Phil Jarvis, Vice President, National Life/Work Center, and co-author of *The Blueprint for Life/Work Designs*

"As a career counselor who specializes in helping women find better ways to blend work and family, I am convinced that a woman's relationship with her husband often is a key element in her career success and job satisfaction. Dr. Block does a masterful job of helping couples. This book will definitely be a recommended read for my clients."
—Nancy Collamer, M.S., career counselor and author

"The ability to balance the responsibilities of a stressful and demanding job with the equally demanding responsibilities of a relationship requires that executives understand their emotional intelligence and posses a variety of interpersonal skills—all to be found in Dr. Block's book!"
—Dr. Kathy Weiss, superintendent of schools, Baldwin, New York

"As a strategic planning consultant whose work takes me on the road nearly every week, *The Marriage-Work Connection* offers new insights and concrete advice on developing and implementing the most critical business plan of my life—how to ensure my role as husband and father is not drowned out by the day-to-day pressures of work and the frequent absences while on the road. It is a book I look forward to turning to frequently when at home and on the road."
—Mitch Horowitz, director of strategy, Battelle Technology Partnership Practice

"Joel Block's book, *The Marriage-Work Connection* brings vigor and relevance to help executives become more effective partners and lovers. An intriguing blend of business acumen and psychological insight, this book provides guidance for anyone wishing to strengthen their marital commitment. It is an engaging invitation to bring the import-ance of relationships to the forefront."
—Anabel L. Jensen, Ph.D., president, Six Seconds Emotional Intelligence Organization

"The fundamentals about responsibility and commitment that Joel Block addresses in his book about connecting as a couple are the same core principles that I teach in the world of trading and finance. If your marriage isn't working, follow the ten steps recommended and create the relationship that you really want and deserve."
—Dr Van K Tharp, author of *Trade Your Way to Financial Freedom*, and world-renowned coach for traders, www.iitm.com

The Marriage-Work Connection

A Couple's Guide to Balancing Your Life Together

DR. JOEL D. BLOCK

CITADEL PRESS
Kensington Publishing Corp.
www.kensingtonbooks.com

CITADEL PRESS BOOKS are published by

Kensington Publishing Corp.
850 Third Avenue
New York, NY 10022

Copyright © 2005 Pop Psych Literary, Inc.

All rights reserved. No part of this book may be reproduced in any form or by any means without the prior written consent of the publisher, excepting brief quotes used in reviews.

Previously published in a hardcover edition under the title *Making It Work When You Work a Lot*.

All Kensington titles, imprints, and distributed lines are available at special quantity discounts for bulk purchases for sales promotions, premiums, fund-raising, educational, or institutional use. Special book excerpts or customized printings can also be created to fit specific needs. For details, write or phone the office of the Kensington special sales manager: Kensington Publishing Corp., 850 Third Avenue, New York, NY 10022, attn: Special Sales Department; phone 1-800-221-2647.

CITADEL PRESS and the Citadel logo are Reg. U.S. Pat. & TM Off.

Interior design by Rachel Reiss

First printing: October 2005
First trade paperback printing: October 2006
10 9 8 7 6 5 4 3 2 1

Printed in the United States of America

Library of Congress Control Number: 2005928508

ISBN 0-8065-2762-5

My Family and Friends:
The rest is decoration

Contents

Author's Note — x

Introduction — 1

Part I: Current Market Conditions — 13
- Strategy One: Success Begins with Commitment — 15
- Strategy Two: Unite, Don't Divide — 32
- Strategy Three: Develop a Culture of Collaboration — 48

Part II: Marketing Plan and Sales Strategy — 69
- Strategy Four: Create Lasting Value — 71
- Strategy Five: Become a Skillful Communicator — 91
- Strategy Six: Build on Strengths — 110
- Strategy Seven: Grow Your Children Effectively — 130

Part III: Long-Term Development Plan — 145
- Strategy Eight: Protect Your Investment — 147
- Strategy Nine: Periodically Assess Progress — 160
- Strategy Ten: Maximize Resources — 167

Part IV: Best Practices — 183
- The Ten Power Strategies Action Plan — 185

Afterword: Memo to the CEO — 197

Bibliography — 201

Index — 203

About the Author — 211

Author's Note

The identities of the people described herein were protected by altering names and various other external characteristics; the essential psychological and social dynamics involved have been preserved. Any resemblance to real persons is strictly intentional; any identification of particular persons is, I trust, impossible.

The terms "husband and wife," "him and her," and "relationship and marriage," require clarification. Often the conventional "him" was used because it is awkward to say "him or her" each time I referred to an individual whose gender was inconsequential; so, too, the use of "wife," "husband," "spouse," and "marriage" is not meant to exclude unmarried readers, male or female. Indeed, it is my hope that the discussion in this book will prove helpful to any two people engaged in an ongoing love relationship.

The Marriage-Work Connection

Introduction

Coming Home Empty

When a business organization employs a married executive, it has engaged not one but two people, the executive and his or her spouse. It is rare, however, for organizational leaders to consider the executive's marriage, even though the spouse indirectly becomes part of the organization.

This is a shortsighted approach. Executive marriages are becoming an endangered species and when they are not protected, the cost to families as well as to the corporate culture is steep. In fact, troubled marriages and divorce ruin more executives than business failure.

The New York Times in a front-page story Sunday, September 5, 2004, reported that sixty-two percent of American workers say their workload has increased and fifty-three percent say work leaves them "overtired and overwhelmed." Executives often bear the brunt of increased responsibility and, as the article states, are particularly at risk because they tend to take their work home. It is enough to stress family life to the limit—and it does. In particular, the stress of the exec work style undermines our marriages.

Yes, there are men and women who are successful in the corporate world and in married life. But they are becoming more the exception than the rule. For example, Jacqueline Strayer, vice president of corporate communications at Arrow Electronics, an electronic-parts distributor, stated in the *Wall Street Journal* (March 29, 2004), "I have always brought my work life into my home, and had my husband and son participate in what I am doing...I think when you involve your family in this way, it becomes part of the fabric of your whole life, it is not compartmentalized."

Aside from being a high-level executive, mom, and wife, Ms. Strayer is completing work toward a doctorate. It appears as if Ms. Strayer is beating the odds by doing well on all fronts. Unfortunately, her experience is not commonplace. It's not just the amount of work we have; it's the psychological characteristics of our positions that are also troublesome. For the typical executive with an emotionally demanding job, one marked by high pressure and a boss who provides little or no support, the likely impact is marital tension, a trio of New York researchers reports in the *Journal of Marriage and the Family.* (Vol. 54, No. 1)

Execs in such jobs have an excess of marital arguments about a wide range of topics, from finances to how to spend their leisure time. Job-generated pressure hampers their ability to meet family demands and creates a negative mood at work that spills over into home life. Negative moods generated on the job make workers psychologically unavailable at home—preoccupied with work, fatigued, and irritable. When thinking about work, they are not able to pay attention to their spouses. Staying happily married is the executive Achilles heel and it is not getting any better.

For two-career couples and single parents, nonstandard schedules make child care complex. Nearly a third of extended-hours employees have children under eighteen. More than a quarter of employed women regularly work nights, evenings, and weekends, when quality care is least available. Women are struggling with the question, What do you do with your kids? And there are no great solutions, adding to the strain on marriages.

Carl E. Van Horn, a professor of public policy at Rutgers and an authority on the history of work in the United States, told Congress, after having completed a national survey, that workers were generally satisfied with their jobs but considered "the ability to balance work and family as more important than any other job factor, including job security and salary." (*New York Times*, September, 19, 2004)

In another *New York Times* article, this one appearing on Sunday, January 4, 2004, right after the New Year, Jim Jenkins, the president of Creative Visions Consulting, an executive coaching firm based in Frederick, Maryland, said he was "swamped" with calls from high-powered executives looking for help in carrying out their New Year's resolutions.

What were their resolutions? Mr. Jenkins said that in addition to finding a way to spend more time with their family, he has been getting more calls from overworked executives who want to "reignite the flame" with their spouses.

The pressure is being felt by nearly everyone. It is, for example, no news for working mothers that their ordinary work pressures are compounded by the mental strain of being on call for unexpected family problems, like a sick child. Single and married mothers alike, it has been found (*Psychosomatic Medicine* 59, 1977), have higher levels of cortisone, the stress hormone, than do their counterparts in the workplace who do not have children at home. What's more, women executives are more likely than women in a junior position to have an alcohol problem, according to a study published in the journal *Occupational Environmental Medicine*.

The issue of work stress colliding with marriage and family life resonates so strongly that it has hit the media in various forms. Novels, cartoon strips, ads, and TV shows poke fun at people who tip the scales toward work, making them less effective at home.

In a new and yet to be syndicated comic strip, "CEO Dad," Tom Stern, a Los Angeles executive recruiter, lampoons his work-obsessed hero's clumsy attempts to relate to his family with authoritarian corner-office tactics.

In a painfully funny new British novel, *I Don't Know How She Does It* by Allison Pearson, frazzled heroine Kate Reddy neglects her kids and nearly wrecks her marriage in her frenzy to succeed at her investment-management job. In another novel, *Moral Hazards* by Kate Jennings, the heroine takes a Wall Street job to pay for care for her ailing husband, creating a darkly funny contrast of corporate infighting with the life-and-death realities she faces at home.

Work-family stress is also at the heart of several TV sitcoms. "The Office," a daring, unflinching take on workplace tensions, became the most popular sitcom on British television. An American version premiered in 2005 on NBC. On another American sitcom, "Life with Bonnie," a talk-show host "creatively balances family commitments and career obligations using sincerity and humor," ABC says in publicity materials.

In real life, the impact of an executive's lifestyle on home life is not usually funny. Not long ago, I had breakfast with four top-level execs from different corners of the country, three of whom were on the road more than they were at home. Each of the men, in the understated manner of those accustomed to putting out fires, spoke of their grueling schedules and the cost their lifestyle had taken on their home life.

Two out of the three were on second marriages that were failing. Both of them volunteered that the complaints they heard from their wives were echoes of those from their previous marriage and they could not deny the legitimacy. The third executive, concerned, but not as experienced at picking up the cues of end-stage marital unhappiness, wrote me that he was served with divorce papers when he arrived home.

The lone woman in the group, whose travel schedule was minimal but whose office hours were nearly endless, earned three times what her stay-at-home-dad husband had earned when he was in the workforce. She described her marriage as stable but unsatisfactory, wryly commenting that it seemed as if her husband's libido plummeted each time her income increased. She had no idea how to overcome her unconventional role reversal.

Her parting comment gave voice to the discouragement she labored with: "It's not as if I can put together a plan by networking with others that share my circumstance. They're doing as badly or worse in their marriages!" She looked to the men around the table and added, "Your wives sound like they're also clueless. Whether they lead fast-track lives or not, we're all struggling at home."

The thinking that led to this book has many roots, but the conversation that morning was definitely a catalyst. It became all too clear that executives, usually on solid footing in the workplace, were stumbling on the homefront.

It is no wonder. Business has moved away from traditional employment, where if you simply did your job, you'd have a job. Now, as reported in the *Times* article of September 5, four out of ten Americans work at nonstandard times and executives, regardless of shift, are putting in more hours. The odd hours include evenings, nights, rotating shifts, and weekends to meet the demands of global supply chains in every time zone. To make the distinction between work and non-work hours even fuzzier, home life is invaded by technology (e.g., Blackberries, cell phones, and laptops) that acts like a virtual leash.

Add rising health care costs, concerns about downsizing, or other factors that make job security iffy, and we end up with what one executive I spoke with calls "the work ethic of fear." It is apparent to nearly everyone, especially those of us on the executive fast track: modern life is a rush and we have created an office culture where too much work is not enough.

We are all going at a fast pace and seldom take the time to examine our lives. We become strangers to ourselves and to our families, climbing the ladder of success without pausing to reflect on whether the destination we are heading toward is the place we want to be. And even if we want to be where we are, the demands of work leave us coming home on empty.

Education for Life

Our educational system is of little help; we learn about every subject but ourselves and how to relate to others. What's more, most of us are so caught up in being successful in the conventional sense that we stride past questions like *What really matters to me? Where am I going in my personal life? Who loves me and whom do I love? What are my intrinsic criteria for success?* Without awareness of our values we remain confused about what we really believe in, what we live for.

In the rush and pressure of our workdays, our attention is focused on tasks, completing the immediate and planning the implementation of the next one. It takes a mental pause, which rarely occurs, to reflect on the subterranean flow of mood. Our feelings are always with us, but typically we are not in touch with our feelings. We can't overcome our conflicts or develop ourselves emotionally and relationship-wise without stopping long enough to strip away our "positions" and "policies," getting down to what really matters.

Often, it is not until our feelings boil and spill over that we pay attention. By then, everything is compounded. Stress at home added to work stress doesn't equal two units of stress, it equals an amount that is barely manageable.

Not living our lives in harmony with and attuned to who we really are can be disastrous. The choices we make will profoundly influence and shape us over time. If our choices are at odds with our core values, it is very likely that our lives will be less joyous, and may, in fact, become quite lonely.

The facts:
- Execs find marital bliss harder to achieve than success in business.
- Ego and opportunity ruin executive marriages.
- Interests and activities shared by couples fall off as execs rise to more responsible job levels.
- Executive divorce comes at enormous cost.

It's the sensational divorces that make the headlines: *General Electric* CEO Jack Welch leaving his second wife Jane; former *Ford* CEO Jacques Nasser's marriage with Jennifer falling apart; Anna Murdoch and *Multi Media* CEO Rupert Murdoch splitting; Sumner Redstone, CEO of *Viacom*, and Phyllis calling it quits. In each instance, the CEO's accumulated wealth became a battleground and included emotional costs that were prohibitive.

For the millions of executives who have not grabbed the CEO ring, personal lives are crumbling as well, if more quietly. Divorce statistics are skyrocketing. It's clear, more than half of us are not only bad at marriage, we're also lousy at divorce. We're still doing it in record numbers, but we don't seem to be learning from the experience—60 percent of second marriages fail as well.

After we recover from the failure and pick up the shattered family pieces, we still don't know how to make relationships work. The execs that form the backbone of our nation's businesses are a unique group of highly intelligent, driven, accomplished men and women whose work lives are soaring while their personal lives are crashing.

Many executive wives, "widows" whose husbands are not dead, just absent, are raising the children alone since their rising star husbands are rarely home. Other couples are climbing the corporate ladder together (in the country club locker room, this is sometimes called the DINS marriage: Double Income, No Sex). In growing numbers a different marital arrangement is forming, sometimes called SAHD (Stay at Home Dads), in which men are raising the children and mourning their diminished testosterone while women are increasing theirs and fighting for the corner office.

Women who earn more than their husbands—more than one in three working wives nationwide—are losing them in droves. The surveys say otherwise, but in my in-depth discussions, it is evident that most men simply cannot adjust to not being the primary breadwinners.

Although Ozzie and Harriet have long since died as icons of our intimate arrangements, the notion that they symbolized—that it's a husband's duty to bring home the bacon—lives on, whether we are aware of it or not, having been absorbed from the culture before we ever gave much thought to gender roles.

So when a woman brings home the bacon, family dynamics may take a turn for the worse as conventional identities and gender-role expectations are jumbled. Often, couples deny that this is a problem, insisting that their arguments are over other issues.

Typically, when faced with this situation, a man will say and do things that diminish his wife. He sees his partner as "the opponent." He finds fault with her in order to feel better about himself. He may act hostile without directly attributing his behavior to his anger over his wife's earning power. If he doesn't openly sabotage his wife's success through an affair or other assault, he may do it in more subtle ways, like refusing to do his share of housework and child care, or failing to give an appropriate response to his spouse's success, such as offering congratulations or support.

Indeed, many female execs, high achievers who end up in senior management, suffer from relationship deprivation. Their connections become function-based, goal-oriented, and more characteristic of the patterns of the typical man. Not to be left out, in growing numbers male execs moving into their late forties, having spent their highly pressured careers ignoring their inner lives, are waking up to find themselves in the midst of personal crises.

Heating things up, extramarital affairs among execs, both men and women, have become commonplace and, ironically, everyone is complaining that there is no time for relationships. Affairs have become such a part of office culture that *Newsweek* featured the phenomenon in a cover story, "The New Infidelity: From Office Affairs to Internet Hookups." (July 12, 2004) Add alcohol and heavy travel schedules to the mix and the handwriting is on the boardroom wall: *Executive marriage is in crisis!*

Getting married to an exec can fill a person with hope. Staying married to an exec is an altogether different matter, requiring special competencies. Execs and their spouses need a *portable relationship coach* that speaks exec language—succinct, sensible, and practical.

This book is a real-life action plan with the mission of protecting executive marriages. It was formulated after interviews with nearly one hundred executives and their spouses, men and women from across the country. The volunteers acted as an informal focus group so that the issues addressed in this volume are truly representative of the exec lifestyle.

Each chapter is derived from the expressed concerns of execs struggling to make their marriages work and, as a review of the table of contents reveals, the issues they raised involve competencies that are also crucial in the world of business. Not only will this assist the exec spouse in communicating in a language familiar to his or her partner, the principles herein will also notch up exec performance on the job as well as on the home front.

Throughout, commentary and research from the organizational world will highlight how the marriage-strengthening principles discussed here have a direct relationship with smart business tactics.

Do you have a spouse who is resistant to working on the marriage? Use the association between savvy business tactics and solid marriages to make your case.

Two recent studies by the Center for Creative Leadership reported by Voight in the Wall Street Online piece have found that executives who make more time for family and other out-of-work activities are rated higher in work performance by bosses and colleagues than those pulling all-nighters in the office. Researchers found that as well as the emotional recharge these activities give, the skills developed out-of-hours are transferable to the office. "How to negotiate, listening skills, interpersonal skills dealing with in-laws or stepchildren, these are all valuable in the office," says Marian Ruderman, the center's director of research.

Without question, the positive spillover—skills honed at home—have enormous benefits. Execs who bring marriage-strengthening competencies to the office and apply them with employees will notch up their success dramatically. At 3M, for example, a program designed to lower health costs was constructed so that it bolstered resiliency competencies for employees both at work and at home.

The program worked because the developers had the foresight to realize that a good day at work is more than erased by a home life that is deteriorative of health and well-being. In fact, researchers are quick to point out that an emotionally troubled home life is not only on the short list of factors that lower productivity of executives but it will also cut their lives short.

The cost of ignoring the relationship-strengthening principles herein is evident in the story of an extraordinarily well-credentialed vice-president at one of our countries largest food companies who had hit a promotion ceiling because of his poor relational skills.

Unsociable, introverted, he was more comfortable sending memos than using face-to-face contact. In meetings he was rude, controlling, and combative. One can only guess what his home life was like. He was either married to a saint, or living alone in a cave somewhere. In any case, a coach was brought in to help the VP on an intense one-to-one basis that lasted for months until he got it; it was only then that his career began to move forward once again.

The point is very simple: Ignoring emotional competency puts you at greater risk for a shattered home life and for developing an artificial career ceiling of your own construction.

The Bottom Line

I am a psychologist specializing in couple relationships and I have also been an executive.

As a couples therapist I have successfully treated hundreds of devastated exec marriages over the years, giving rise to my desire to formulate a plan that addresses the challenges unique to these relationships.

The plan is focused on the bottom line: strategies for maintaining the vitality and energy of love in executive marriages. It features real-life stories:

> We'll hear from Marion, who has a 10-percent marriage. Her husband is on the road 80 percent of the time and catches up on sleep half of the time he is at home. She uses innovative techniques to save her marriage.

> We'll get to know Eleanor, whose answer to the stress of her husband's tension-filled lifestyle is champagne, at the rate of two bottles a day. Her story does not have a happy ending.

> Joyce thought she had an answer as well. The neglect and resentment she felt as a result of Paul's extraordinary work schedule was temporarily eased by her fling with a former colleague of hers. She confessed her infidelity to Paul—and they're still together! We'll hear about repair strategies that are tried and proven.

> And Rob, a stay at home dad, has also considered soothing his ego by having an affair. He's come up with a better solution, one that saved his marriage as well as his ego.

> Kevin has developed an intriguing method for keeping Janice at a distance. We'll see how Janice reacted and what they did to bring value back to their relationship.

> Alex and Florence have something to offer as well. Alex badgered Florence about her housekeeping and then acknowledged that wasn't the issue at all. His beef was with Florence's meteoric career progression, especially since his career was stalling. Unlike many other couples where the wife is the bigger earner, Florence and Alex worked things out brilliantly.

These are mere samplings of real-life stories behind the curtain in the exec suite. There is also the pressure of meeting the expenses in an upscale neighborhood, becoming a member of the "in" club, socializing with the right people, and the drama of doing whatever else is necessary to succeed in a dog-eat-dog world.

Very often, all this comes at a cost that is paid by having to sit down with a divorce lawyer to divide assets that have been accumulated over years of hard work. Of course, divorce lawyers do not and cannot address the broken hearts that have littered the highway of success.

Here's the no-brainer: Hardly anything else in an exec's life will have as profound an impact as a marriage under assault, touching everything, including the exec's work performance.

Consider this statement from Lynne Z. Gold-Biken, chair of the family law department of the Philadelphia-based law firm Wolf, Block, Schorr and Solis-Cohen LLP:

> Corporate America needs to be aware of the impact of divorce on their bottom line. Just as abuse has an impact on the bottom line of a corporation, so does divorce. The HR department ought to be providing communication skills and [similar] courses for executives so they can make their marriages better and stronger. Because it really is in the interest of the corporation to keep marriages together. Divorce costs them a lot of money, for many reasons: time, productivity, bad publicity. But I'm very serious about these communication skills. When people start getting in trouble with their partners, if they know there's a place, as part of their perks, that they can go to for [counseling and help], it would cut down on the divorce rate, which would obviously cut down on this problem. (March 2003, p. 64)

Emotional Savvy

Here's the hard reality: while marriage can be difficult under any circumstances, maintaining a successful executive marriage is like walking a high wire. For that reason there is no discussion of pre-nups, nor is there a chapter titled "You're Fired: Exit Strategies." Neither of these topics is covered because the best way to walk the exec marriage high wire is without a net.

Going in with thoughts of taking a dive is negative. What's more, it's been my observation that those walking the wire with a net are likely to be short on the commitment it takes to meet the challenge. We are all familiar with businesses that fail due to lack of focus and commitment. The same is true in our personal lives.

If we are going to succeed at home, the challenge requires that we smarten up, but not in the usual sense; what matters is a different way of being smart. We need to bring emotional intelligence to our personal life. Emotional intelligence, it has been demonstrated repeatedly and convincingly, is the key to success in the business world. This book brings the powerful skills of emotional intelligence to marital life.

It is especially critical because a struggling marriage is on the short list of circumstances that will not only deter peak performance, and significantly increase vulnerability to health problems, it will also impact our children more than any other factor in their daily lives.

What's more, being anxious, always in a rush and racing after whatever it is we've imagined will help us to be more at peace with ourselves, is like running to catch the shadow of a passing cloud on a hot summer's day so that we get to stand in a cool spot!

Rushing through our lives does not produce more time, or do one thing to increase productivity. To the contrary, rushing limits possibilities by restricting our focus and often relegating our personal life to the "tomorrow" box.

We live in a time when our prospects increasingly depend on managing ourselves and handling our relationships more artfully. My hope is to offer some practical strategies for the crucial personal challenges we all face in an ever-demanding business culture.

Instead of quick fixes, which look slick but ultimately disappoint, you will find in the pages that follow sound guidelines for the real work of becoming skilled at the business of marriage. We'll learn from the mistakes of those who are on the wrong track, and hear from others, execs and their spouses, who have made their relationships successful.

As executives, we value responsibility; it is one of our defining characteristics. Bear this in mind: *The ultimate act of responsibility at work is taking control of your own state of mind when you return home. That is how you become the author of your life.*

PART I:
■■■■■■■

Current Market Conditions

STRATEGY ONE

Success Begins with Commitment

Anatomy of a Failing Relationship

The scene is an exclusive seaside restaurant. A couple in their mid-forties is having dinner. Paul, the senior vice-president of a financial investment firm, is deeply tanned and prosperous looking. Joyce, just having returned to work as a model, has bright green eyes and a lightly freckled face under a fluff of reddish-brown hair. Paul and Joyce Wilson have been married eighteen years.

This night, as on many others, their attention is directed elsewhere. Presently their eyes and ears are trained on a younger couple seated nearby, a man and woman locked in each other's gaze, speaking softly, inaudibly, sometimes laughing together, other times looking very serious, playful, and earnest, all the while holding hands.

Paul and Joyce, disconnected for many years, share a silent thought: We were that couple in the early years. When did the bottom fall out?

The bottom, of course, did not suddenly fall out. Relationships do not abruptly collapse. Life is a process. Relationships don't break; they slowly melt. The Wilsons, who once thought they had it made, failed or refused to recognize the signals, flashing over nearly two decades, telling them that they hadn't.

Relationships crumble, finally, when each partner is locked into blaming the other for failing to live up to the original vision that impelled the alignment: "I thought you were going to accept me just the way I was."

Social science has a name for that fading dynamic—it is called *disillusionment*. Lovers initially put their best foot forward, ignoring or rationalizing each other's shortcomings. After they tie the knot, idealized images begin to give way to more realistic ones. This often leads to disappointment, loss of love, and ultimately for too many of us, distress and divorce.

We begin our journey drawn to the familiar, and choose a partner who reminds us of significant people from our childhood—usually our parents. Unwittingly, we set out to re-create the patterns of our childhood. Dreaming of love, we join together out of the barely fortified hope that our fantasies will spring to life. But lasting love is an altogether different venture requiring a definite skill set.

The Wilsons, like many of us, began with the dream of love and not much more. Although Paul and Joyce are highly intelligent and well educated, they were naïve and ill-informed when it came to the competencies and realities of maintaining a long-term relationship balanced with challenging careers.

Neither understood the need for being "relationship educated," since the state of being in love was supposed to automatically ensure a happy, vital union. Though unrealistic, it's not an uncommon position, especially in a first union.

As they grew through adulthood together, there were no mentors to tell them that marriage, involving two complex and ever-changing individuals and, later, equally complex and rapidly changing children, precludes continuous and perfect harmony, or that economic conditions, work pressures, illness, in-laws, and aging would influence and stress their relationship. Although commonplace, no models existed for their dual-career marriage or for Paul's obsession with work when Joyce gave up her modeling career to raise their children.

Each confirmed for the other the mistaken notion that "every day things will get better and better." In reality, nothing could be further from the truth. Problems at the beginning of marriage worsen over time rather than get better, as many couples expect. Rather than viewing differences and conflicts as a sign of incompatibility, couples need to see them as opportunities for developing skills that they can use for the rest of their lives together.

Considering the demands we put on this fragile bond—heightened sexual passion, continuous love, emotional security, stimulating companionship, thorough compatibility—it is no wonder that some two-fifths of all divorce actions are initiated during the first two years of marriage.

The collision with reality was not immediate for the Wilsons. They were sheltered by intense infatuation during their courtship, and by the demands and pressures of family life in the beginning years of their marriage. In our conversation about their marriage, Joyce recalls:

After the fourth year of marriage our son was born. I worked for another two years but it was too stressful for all of us so I stopped modeling and settled into the life of the suburban domesticate—chief cook, bottle washer, chauffeur, and occasional tennis player. I was very involved in parenting, community affairs, and house ownership. Paul worked with tenacity and single-mindedness to put himself through college. Working by day in a brokerage firm, going to school at night and all summer, he lived on four hours of sleep a night for weeks at a time.

Without taking a breath after he got his bachelor's degree, Paul continued and earned his MBA. By then he was very successful in the financial investment business. Unfortunately, though, we really didn't get to know each other; both of us were too consumed in our own worlds. I was absorbed in my own career and later I was at home with two preschoolers and was not particularly interested in Paul's business activities. He had a similar disinterest in, or even distaste for my domestic posture.

During these early years, the Wilsons had a marriage that was comfortable but only minimally companionable. Although they were pleasant with each other, their interests, goals, and life views were gradually diverging.

What's more, to stabilize her marriage, Joyce had sacrificed her career, which was not without risk. A wife who drops out of the workforce and stays out for a long time will probably never make up for that lost economic ground when she returns to work. Worse, if her husband's income starts to slip—and it did in Paul's case, as we'll see—the couple may be in trouble, both financially and emotionally.

As life became more complicated, discussions exploring beliefs, inner feelings, likes and dislikes, and plans for the future became almost nonexistent between the Wilsons. In striking contrast to the enthusiasm of courtship, conversation at times was painfully strained.

Paul commented to me:

Joyce and I had at least two essentials that seem important for a good marriage: We respected each other, and we were attracted to each other sexually. That should have been enough. But it wasn't; there was a large, hollow gulf in between our sexual contacts. There was only a minimum of talk; and what there was, more often than not, involved the basic family functions: "Did you pick up milk?" "Who's driving Kevin to soccer?" "Did anyone call?"

Indeed, a large-scale research effort conducted through Cornell University revealed that the average parents of preschool children talk to each other only about half as much per day as they did during their first intimate years of marriage. This in itself is not necessarily corrosive; the dwindling quantity is minor compared to the painful change of quality.

Researchers found conversation, once spiced with exchanges about books, ideas, and personal relationships, became almost entirely concerned with routine affairs, just as Paul described. "Was there anything in the mail?" "The plumber came to fix the sink." In effect, husbands and wives were using the casual, more mundane words of dispassionate roommates rather than the warm and intimate words of lovers, not sometimes, but most of the time.

After the Wilsons coasted in their unsatisfactory but stable marriage for several years, financial setbacks produced the first real open conflict between them. This was a stormy and bitter period; it was especially hard for Paul to acknowledge and openly deal with conflict. Rather than viewing disagreement as inevitable, Paul did what many men do in the face of strong emotions from a woman: he withdrew.

Men and women handle conflict in radically different ways that subvert the relationship. Men flee, women fight; and they stay stuck in this pattern. Some researchers now believe that men simply have more difficulty than women in handling conflict—a result of early experiences, gender stereotyping, and physiology. Men get emotionally flooded more easily.

Against this backdrop, distress mounted. From Joyce's experience:

Paul had formed a partnership, and his company really began to move. He found out later on that his partner was a thief—stealing funds, gambling, using poor judgment and, as a result, within two years we were broke. I found out that we had lost everything when Paul told me we had to sell the house. I was enraged that we were in this insecure position and that Paul hadn't informed me of what was going on. I reacted to his mismanagement by going back to work. Although I didn't earn nearly as much as I did at the height of my career, I did better than Paul and let him know at every opportunity. Paul, feeling emasculated, used credit cards to make expensive purchases we couldn't pay for. It was as if he were saying, "I'll show you I'm still boss around here." But he wouldn't engage me in any substantive discussion of these things. In response, I did something that I regret to this day, and it hurt him terribly.

The Tipping Point

Paul was overwhelmed by Joyce's emotions and avoided any conflict with her. She responded by trying to re-engage him, advancing as he withdrew, setting up an escalating pattern of anger and frustration. If the pursuer-distancer pattern were not bad enough, other factors conspired to exacerbate this heightening war between Paul and Joyce.

Once pleased by their passionate love life, they became the poster couple of the DINS set (Double Income, No Sex). Their continued limited shared activities—dining out, going to a movie—ceased to provide the enjoyment it had in the past. Communication became even more difficult; Joyce now found herself screaming at Paul almost daily as a result of her growing frustration and alienation.

As displeasing behaviors proliferated, their overall satisfaction with the relationship plummeted. Both felt a loss of commitment, an inability to feel positive, and each awaited the other's move to repair the marriage.

At some point, as occurs with many couples juggling high-stress, demanding lives, Paul and Joyce turned to the latest books about work-life balance, tried organizing their time, fantasized about a dramatic shift in their careers or lifestyle, discussed taking up meditation or New Age "spiritual" teachings. None of it worked; their relationship continued to deteriorate.

And then there was the increasingly common, dramatic, marriage-devastating affair. Joyce, in a voice laced with remorse, gave her accounting to me:

> I had this nagging guilt. My deception and betrayal really bothered me. Although Paul and I were feeling completely disconnected, another involvement was obviously not a solution. To make matters worse, there were a number of underhanded things I noticed myself doing to ease my discomfort. For example, Paul would come home and I would provoke fights. What I really wanted was for Paul to say, "You son of a bitch, go to hell!" Something that would relieve me of my responsibility. This way I could say to myself, "Well, we're *really* on the outs; the old rules are null and void."
>
> The problem is that as bad as things were between us, Paul never got to the point where he was ready to make some terminal-type statement. He wouldn't talk to me, but I couldn't get him to give up on me! Somehow I got to the point where I couldn't continue sneaking around. It happened like this: We were at this party and Michael

Fields was there. He's an ad exec I met at the modeling agency. I said to Paul, "I want to leave; let's get out of here. There's something I have to talk to you about." He said, "What's wrong?" and I told him we'd discuss it on the way home. As we drove away from the party, I told him about my affair with Michael.

His face flushed in a real scary sort of way and his voice cracked as he asked me a lot of questions. Then he sort of curled up within himself and suffered in silence. He was so hurt and so deeply unhappy, I couldn't handle it. Neither could he. We survived, but it left quite a scar on both of us.

The Challenge

The experience of Paul and Joyce Wilson highlights some of the ingredients of relationship distress, particularly with execs who work long hours, bring their work home, and count on their marriage being low maintenance. Many of us are at just such an impasse with the man or woman in our life, wherein a state of slow (or sometimes hastened) erosion is occurring. The process is characterized by a staleness that is reminiscent of a career that has stalled. As was the case with Paul and Joyce, a stalled marital relationship is vulnerable to infidelity—by women as well as men.

The double standard implies that boys will be boys, but girls are supposed to behave properly. Not anymore. Much has changed since Emma Bovary chose suicide with arsenic over living her life branded an adulteress, humiliated, impoverished, and stripped of her romantic ideals and dignity. Today, *Sex and the City*, movies like *Unfaithful*, and a myriad of magazine articles and novels have made every imaginable sex act fodder for cocktail party conversation. Women who are adulterers are no longer tragic figures to be scorned or stoned. When Carmela on the HBO series *The Sopranos* took a lover after putting up with her husband, Tony's, antics over the years, audiences gave her a standing ovation.

It is not that affairs are a media event without a big following in reality. In *Newsweek*'s cover story on this made-for-Hollywood issue, "The New Infidelity," they report that couples therapists estimate the number of women who have had sex outside their marriage is close to 40 percent, compared with 50 percent of men, and the gap is almost certainly closing.

Are these startling figures accurate? It's hard to say, because when people talk about sex in various studies from the less formal to the rigorously controlled, results vary wildly. Men, not surprisingly, amplify their sexual experience, while women minimize it.

Despite the unreliability of the numbers, the trend is clear. With more women in the workforce—nearly sixty percent of women work outside the home—temptation and opportunity are more likely to collide. That has certainly been the trend I have witnessed over nearly three decades working with couples.

One thing is certain: While the development of an enduring relationship provides a degree of emotional fulfillment not afforded by other options in life, it is also more demanding and fraught with more perils and temptations on busy, fully engaged exec lives than most of us realize. When a lover gives a woman everything her husband doesn't—compliments, jewelry, flowers and love notes, along with that most important and seductive factor, his time and attention—the affair becomes difficult to resist.

Men, too, feel bored, unfulfilled, neglected, and pressured by their overscheduled lives. The thrill of being with someone new, whether it be an office romance or an Internet flirtation that makes him feel sexy and alive, can be a powerful lure.

Once an affair has begun, it only serves to further erode intimacy between the married couple. Intimacy requires honesty, openness, and self-disclosure. The deception that accompanies an affair makes this impossible. In addition, if the affair partner becomes the confidante for the husband or wife, someone with whom they can discuss problems in the marriage, the extramarital involvement can be even more threatening to the marriage because it creates a bond of friendship between the affair partners that goes beyond sex.

None of this signals the demise of a fulfilling marriage. However, despite the spate of relationship books promising enduring love, there is no easy path in today's mobile, I-can-have-it-all environment. A long-term relationship must be thought of as alive; as with any living entity, including a business venture, it is constantly evolving, changing as it develops. Keeping ahead of the curve is essential.

While all marriages go through this obstacle-lined change process, executives may not possess the patience to deal with the problems. Their sentiment, if given voice, is something like, "Honey, I'm really, really busy, give me a pass..." Unfortunately, when that sentiment has become a mantra for the long term, it doesn't play well.

Affairs, chronic arguing, and eventual divorce are not inevitabilities, despite the foreboding statistics. We've all seen risky business ventures, those that defy the odds, become hugely successful. But as most exec couples are bound to find, achieving a true and enduring romantic partnership is no small accomplishment. Many of the same elements that bring success to corporate long shots can also be applied to marriage.

The vision, however, better be realistic. As a means of attaining fulfillment for two individuals, a long-term, committed relationship has limitations and imperfections. No other society, to my knowledge, expects so much from such a relationship—the source of all emotional satisfaction—as ours. And few other societies foster such demanding and competitive careers that result in a neglected family life.

Facing this double challenge—formidable emotional demands and too little time—many exec couplings don't work, or they don't work for long. It is likely that a goodly percentage collapse from mere overload.

A satisfying union, one that provides mutual pleasure, requires frequent repair and adjustment and sometimes may even have to undergo a major overhaul. Beyond the chemistry—the attraction between two people that draws them to each other—what does it take to create a vital, lively, and productive relationship?

Perhaps the ingredients for such a coupling cannot be fully accounted for, but neither are they completely elusive. The skill to resolve conflicts with mutual respect must be developed. It is necessary to create new common interests and to keep growing as individuals, both to maximize involvement in shared pleasurable activities and to provide each other with new topics of conversation.

A plan is needed for the division of responsibility that also protects the spousal connection (recall the Wilsons' dilemma: "I was absorbed at home with two preschoolers and was not particularly interested in Paul's business activities. He had a similar disinterest in, or even distaste for, my domestic posture"). Partners need to be able to express their feelings, both positive and negative, in an acceptable manner. A satisfactory degree of trust in the relationship is essential. Emotional safety must be present so that real openness, speaking from the heart, can occur.

There is also the all-important affection factor and mutually satisfying lovemaking. Recall the Wilson's DINS relationship. The problem of low- or no-sex marriages is coming out of the closet. A flurry of recent books, TV coverage, and watercooler talk is drawing new attention to the matter.

Research by Denise Donnelly of Georgia State University, reported in *The Journal of Sex Research*, (30, 1993, 171–179), found that 16 percent of couples fail to have sex at least once a month, a pattern that predicted marital unhappiness and divorce.

Women aren't the only ones refusing sex, either. In her research of married people in sexually inactive marriages, Dr. Donnelly found that in 60 percent of the cases, it was the man who had stopped the sex.

The reasons for low or lack of sex in marriage vary, from extramarital affairs to poor conflict management, child care, fatigue, and job stress. Whatever the cause, here are some suggestions from exec couples I interviewed who have put forth a successful effort to improve their love lives:

- **Keep talking.** All the couples put the issue on their agenda and worked out ways to overcome obstacles. They displayed one of the most powerful characteristics of successful people: persistence. Couples who talk about sexual problems are far more likely to survive than those who don't. This was confirmed in Dr. Donnelly's study. Sexually inactive couples had just given up and stopped talking.
- **Just do it.** With a nod to Nike for this borrowed slogan, the couples I spoke with were realistic about differences in desire and the realities of their busy lives. Consequently, the spouses with lower desire consented to having sex even when they didn't feel like it. That's not as bad as it sounds. First, all of the spouses agreed that they benefited from the closeness, and most of them enjoyed the sexual experience more than they anticipated.
- **Make time.** We all know that if something really matters to us, if it is really important, we find the time. If you were having an affair, you'd find the time. Have an affair with your spouse—and like an affair, set up a time to meet. In our busy lives we can't rely on spontaneity. Synchronize your schedules and make dates with each other. Many couples set a romantic date the same time each week, alternating responsibility for setting the ambiance.
- **Think sex.** Many of the couples realized that their lives were filled with tasks and heavy responsibilities, none of them very sexy. They made an effort to read sexy books, view sexy movies, and permit themselves to have sexy fantasies, all in an effort to make a little shift in attitude and perhaps learn one or two new moves.

Despite the difficulties and obstacles of a life spilling over with necessary tasks on an interminable "to do" list, it is quite possible to revitalize a relationship, to make love last. I have talked with many couples that are doing it, I have done it myself, and I have assisted countless couples in doing it as well. It is eminently attainable!

However, even with authoritative direction, time and effort are required to achieve a desired result. Patience, the courage to change, and the desire to grow are key ingredients. If this sounds like a tall order, consider that it requires more work, energy, strength, and time to support a bad alliance than it does to support a good one. In other words, the cost/benefit analysis suggests that it is foolish to ignore family life: health, well-being, and productivity are at stake.

Where Am I Now?

Even if considerable effort is put forth, the results will be more effective if the effort is well focused and individualized. One size does not fit all. In that regard, what follows is a focused inventory designed to assess where you are now so that you have a clear idea of what you need to accomplish. The inventory is divided into three broad sections:

1. **Support.** This is concerned with behaviors that set the tone of the relationship.
2. **Communication.** This is concerned with the manner in which messages are conveyed.
3. **Conflict resolution.** This is concerned with the manner in which disagreements are handled.

Bear in mind that the function of the inventory is to identify areas where improvement is needed. It is not intended to instigate fault finding. Each item is to be answered independently of the others, and each partner is to take the inventory separately. Base your responses on your feelings over the past few weeks; that is, do not be biased by a particular incident, positive or negative. Instead, consider an overall assessment over a prolonged period.

For each numbered item below, select a description that most accurately describes your relationship. Place the number that corresponds to that description next to each statement. Once you've completed each section, add up the numbers to get your totals.

1	2	3	4
Rarely True	Slightly or occasionally true	Sometimes or moderately true	Almost always true

RELATIONSHIP-ENHANCEMENT INVENTORY

SUPPORT
1. My partner treats me as an equal; he/she promotes the idea that I am worthy of respect.
2. My partner shows appreciation or acknowledges when I do or say something nice.
3. I enjoy spending time with my partner.
4. I am willing, without feeling resentful, to pitch in if my partner needs help to carry out his/her responsibilities.
5. My partner and I do a great deal to express our caring for each other.
6. I make every effort to view my partner's actions in a positive manner.
7. I feel that the effort required to make the relationship work is equitably distributed.

COMMUNICATION
1. I feel understood by my partner when we discuss personal issues.
2. My partner is flexible; he/she is open to new ideas rather than the exclusive pursuit of his/her own point of view.
3. My partner knows when to listen and when to talk during our discussions.
4. I feel that my partner is interested in what I have to say.
5. My partner is open; he/she will reveal personal issues and feelings when the disclosures are likely to advance our discussion.
6. My partner speaks in a manner that is direct and to the point.
7. I can count on my partner's statements as being sincere.

CONFLICT RESOLUTION
1. Discussing disagreements with my partner is productive; irrelevant issues and fault finding do not characterize the conversation.
2. I feel confident that discussions of conflict will not get out of control.
3. The agreements I make with my partner provide clarity as to who was to do what and when.

4. I trust my partner to keep his/her end of an agreement.
5. In general, discussing a disagreement leads to my feeling more hopeful and to identifiable changes in the relationship.
6. I feel I can strongly express my anger when I am distressed.
7. Following a fight, we make up promptly and sincerely rather than carry a prolonged grudge.

INTERPRETATION

If the total score for either partner on any section is twenty-one or less, it is a indication that improvement is necessary. However, low scores should be viewed only as a signal that improvement is recommended, not as proof that the relationship is incurably dysfunctional.

The inventory is not a tested scientific instrument but merely a general guide for determining the need for improvement in each of three particularly important relationship-enhancement areas. In this regard, another assessment should be taken after reading the book and applying the tools herein so that a growth comparison can be obtained.

Little or no positive change in scores should prompt a discussion of specific inventory items that indicate weak areas to be targeted for further improvement.

The Power of Expectation

Not only is it particularly helpful to assess what is needed to improve the spousal relationship, but as with everything else we do in life, attitude is crucial. There is a time-worn tale that in its simplicity has profound implications for interpersonal relationships. A city slicker driving down a country road one evening gets a flat tire. Stranded on this lonely road, he discovers to his consternation that he doesn't have a jack, an absolute necessity if he is to change the tire and be on his way.

Just as he is considering sleeping in the car and seeking help in the morning, he recalls passing a farm a few miles back. "Why not give that a try?" he asks himself. "The weather is mild and I could make it in half an hour." With that, he locks the car and begins to hike.

Once under way, the city slicker starts thinking, "It's late at night, I'll probably wake the farmer, he'll be angry. Farmers don't like city folks, he'll be nasty...he probably won't trust me to bring back his jack anyway...I can just see this guy sneering at me, saying to himself, 'That dumb city slicker, doesn't even know enough to keep a jack in his car!'" With that final thought, he arrives at the farmer's house, calls out, and the farmer opens his window. Before the farmer can utter a word, the city slicker shouts, "You can take your stinkin' jack and shove it!" That night the city slicker sleeps in his car.

All of us are continually rehearsing our reactions to anticipated future events. How we think about what awaits us, particularly in the near future, strongly influences our lives. Hope spurs us on; hopelessness, the inability to anticipate satisfaction, creates despair. Many of us are, in fact, despondent; we view our relationships as floundering and act accordingly, that is to say, with weakened commitment. We put little in because we expect little in return, and this is just what we get, a meager return. As with the city slicker, we expect negativity, communicate our anticipation, and get to "sleep in the car."

In sharp contrast, the hopeful person, expecting that an event will turn out well, signals his enthusiasm through facial expressions, stature, and confident attitude. Those who are involved with this person are encouraged by his display of self-assurance, are drawn in by his enthusiasm, and are likely to respond in kind. The law of expectations is simple: The way an event is viewed (how you expect it to turn out) will affect your behavior and, in turn, alter the actual outcome.

The power of expectation was very evident among supervisors of sailors in the U.S. Navy who were low performers (LPs). Supervisors were given a simple tactic to change the LPs' behavior: expect the best of them, despite their checkered histories. The supervisors took the advice and treated the sailors like winners. The positive expectations proved powerful. The LPs began to do better on every front.

In a similar vein, athletic coaches and good managers alike have long known that one strategy used to boost performance is the combination of a suitable challenge and communicating a belief in the person's ability to perform admirably. Positive imagery, a method for visualizing success in the mind's eye, has long been used in athletics. As the saying goes, imagining yourself succeeding doesn't guarantee a win, but viewing yourself losing almost always guarantees that you'll get what you see.

In another innovative experiment, once again involving interpersonal relationships, researchers wanted to examine the effect of expectations of interpersonal "warmth" and "coldness." How does the expectation that a person will be warm or cold influence actual impressions of that person? How do these expectations influence behavior toward this person? The subjects were sixty-five college students in three college classes. A person unknown to the students was introduced to each class as a temporary replacement for their regular instructor.

Half of the members of each class were given biographical information about the substitute instructor, which included the statement that he was "rather cold." The remaining subjects were independently given identical information, except that it included the statement that the instructor was "very warm."

The instructor led each class in a twenty-minute discussion, and a record was kept of each student's participation. Afterward, first-impression ratings of the instructor were obtained from all students. Comparison of the "warm" and "cold" expectation groups revealed impressions that strongly coincided with their expectations: Those who anticipated a warm instructor described him as more considerate of others, less formal, more social, and more humorous than those who anticipated a cold instructor. Warm "expecters" also participated in the class discussion significantly more than the students given the cold expectation did.

The main theme of these studies (and of others covering such diverse topics as stuttering, psychological testing, and physical disability) is that expectations are major determinants of human behavior; expectations are both interpersonally communicated and influenced by others' behavior. With this material as background, it becomes apparent that negative expectations ("He doesn't care about me and he never will") can become self-fulfilling prophecies.

Taking a Stand

Positive expectations are necessary and being well focused is necessary as well, but neither is sufficient. If you really thought about the human dilemma, it's not a mystery why so many good intentions go the way of New Year's resolutions.

Slipping back into the same old behavior patterns is so commonplace as to be the rule rather than the exception. Whether in the workplace or in front of the fireplace, most of us lug the mental baggage with us that frustrates our desire to be all that we can be. Some of us even devote a good portion of our mental energy to demonizing ourselves for this shortcoming.

We could all do so much more if we could just stick to a worthy goal without letting excuses get the better of us. I'm sure you have either read about or maybe even met some people who are able to pursue their ambition unfettered by distractions of any kind. They are so dedicated to their intentions that they appear to be nothing short of an awe-inspiring force of nature.

To think that they are super-human, or that they didn't have to struggle to stay on course as the rest of us did, is just another excuse. It implies that our struggle is somehow greater than theirs is, therefore we can't expect our success to equal theirs.

The real problem with not sticking to a goal as momentous as strengthening one's marriage is that some of the myriad ways we get off track are disguised. Straightforward resistance ("He doesn't deserve to be treated with consideration") is easier because it is recognizable.

It is the more seductive side-tracks that wield the most power. These range from discouragement that your partner is not meeting you partway, to doubting that your efforts will make a difference, expending your energy complaining, and finding a host of things to do that are not nearly as important as strengthening your personal life.

In contrast, if your dream is to have a marriage that is as exciting as a new business venture, one thing can be said with absolute certainty: Separate yourself from distractions and you will have created the possibility of becoming the unstoppable agent of your intentions.

As I assume you've guessed by now, we are talking about that all-important C word, commitment. Simply said, when you make a commitment you create a pledge to produce a specific result. It's a promise to give your full effort. In contrast to wishful thinking ("I'd love to be happier with my spouse"), commitment is a journey that involves taking action to fulfill your pledge.

Commitment is critical to success. The essence of commitment is making your goals and the goals of your partner one and the same. Just as in organizational life, when goals resonate among team members good things are likely to happen.

Mastering the art of creating and living according to your commitments will be one of the most powerful tools in your tool kit. Like other tools, they have a specific purpose. They are the drivers making things happen that would not otherwise occur. Fulfilled commitments can lead to breakthroughs in every area of life.

If you are thinking that commitment has always been a problem for you, consider that your life is full of commitments. Just look at your married life as it is now. That's exactly what you have been committed to maintaining.

Tool Kit

The first and most important step is that both husband and wife unite as team members.

Find a quiet place, look your partner in the eye, and pledge your commitment to strengthening the marriage. Shake hands on it. Make it a formal agreement. Turning a failing business around requires pulling out the stops; if you are serious about turning your marriage around you'll put the same energy forward.

Bear in mind that fear, uncertainty, and negative expectations block the gate to success. It is natural as you approach the gate to feel these emotions and have these thoughts. The key to the gate is committed action. Here are some things that you can do so that you don't drop the key:

1. Make a list of your major commitment obstacles, the kinds of things that are likely to shoot your dreams out of the sky. Carry the list around with you and glance at it from time to time so that you stave off a sneak attack.
2. Remember that you will fortify your marriage piece by piece. Think of the process as incremental so as not to overwhelm yourself.
3. All created commitments require some degree of faith. You are not making a prediction on past results but proactively authoring the future with your newly committed effort. The whole point of your commitment is to make something happen that cannot be logically inferred based on the past.
4. Minimize your distractions by spending time with people whose marriage is working. Speaking positively about your partner as well as your intention to invigorate your bond will fortify your resolve. This will also help you avoid the slippery slope of listening too intently to that sabotaging inner voice that gets louder when a marriage is struggling. The last thing you need is to join in the chorus of unhappily married couples who are dedicated to having a miserable life together.
5. If you acknowledge your inner voice and you are aware of how sabotaging it can be when a marriage is struggling, then you own it, rather than it owning you. Once you start to recognize the excuses and negative

thinking for what it is, mere static, you have taken some strong steps on the path to freedom.
6. Visualize yourself in the midst of a fulfilling marriage. Picture a scene from that marriage and make it as real and as satisfying as you can. Imagine how you would feel. See if you can make it as real as if it were actually happening. Revisit this visualization as often as possible, particularly if your distractions are planning an attack.
7. Don't be discouraged by setbacks. They are part of the alarm your survival system sets up to let you know you have to stay alert. Feel the fear, experience the discouragement, and go forward.

Discussion Forum

All of us have struggled with commitment in one form or another. Share your list of commitment obstacles (see number 1 above) with your spouse and discuss your plan for overcoming them. Specifically, consider these questions in your overall discussion: How did you overcome obstacles and blind spots in any area of your life that caused difficulty for you in the past? What was the first step you took to accomplish your goal? What was the most important thing you did that contributed to your success?

Post this on your bulletin board:

My commitments will make me the inventor of my future.

STRATEGY TWO

▪▪▪▪▪▪▪▪▪▪

Unite, Don't Divide

The Blame Game

John, a rising star in a biotech venture, wants Eleanor, his wife of seven years, to take more responsibility for running their home and setting up a more structured routine for their two sons, ages four and six. According to Eleanor, when John comes home late in the evening, "He reviews the house like he's doing a military inspection."

John's view contrasts with Eleanor's and is a source of continuing tension between them. "After a long day making decisions that involve millions of dollars, I don't want to come home to chaos. There are toys all around. The dishes are still in the sink and the kids are up too late. You've got to get your act together. It's that simple."

"It's not that simple," Eleanor contends. "These are your children as well! In fact, I purposely rebel. I am an adult, not some child who is going to get a nightly report card!"

Often one of the first things to go in a troubled marriage is politeness. As laughter and validation disappear, criticism and pain build. Attempts to get communication back on track seem useless, and partners give in to hostile and negative thoughts and feelings.

Within a year after these types of exchanges began to escalate, and the arguments spread to include other areas of contention, John began smelling alcohol on Eleanor's breath when he arrived home. He had good reason to pick up the scent of alcohol; Eleanor had begun drinking two bottles of champagne a day. The following year, when I met John and Eleanor, their marriage was already terminal. John was coming home later and angrier; Eleanor was drunk every night. John and Eleanor were divorced in the tenth year of their marriage and continued the blame game in a three-year custody battle.

Research has unequivocally demonstrated that relationships characterized by criticism are bound to end in divorce or unabated distress. In short, if criticism is chronic, especially when it is tainted with sarcasm and contempt, there is no happy ending.

Driven, performance-based men and women set the performance bar high for themselves and usually demand the same of others—especially their marital partners. This is the common type A response, and it has the potential to wreak havoc in intimate relationships. This is us! Current research suggests that at least 70 percent of execs, whether male or female, are type A.

In other words, if you've read that type A behavior, especially the irritability factor, is bad for your health, there's more bad news: It makes having a successful relationship the biggest challenge you'll face!

The reality is that our exec lifestyles have exploded with increased pressures and many roles to fill. We're constantly seeking to balance four areas: commitment to intimate relationships, to familial relationships, to work, and to ourselves.

How are we supposed to keep our marriages going when, as individuals, we're scrambling to keep all these commitments under control, all within the constraints of seven twenty-four-hour days?

The result of trying to fit everything we deem important into the time we have is that invariably execs notch it up. We become even more hard driving, competitive, time urgent, controlling, critical, and, in some instances, hot-tempered. Because we've got much to do and feel it's important to get everything done, high-powered people like us easily become frustrated, irritable, and too often hostile and cynical.

When things don't go our way, we flare up; when we're upset, we act more type A. The irony is that the number one stressor for type As is difficulty tolerating what goes on in close relationships.

Relationship issues are the one area that high-powered people like us aren't fully in control of, nor expert in resolving, in part because our coping style generates tension in relationships. We're accustomed to juggling exceptional amounts of stuff, in effect normalizing abnormal situations, and expect our partners, as we saw with John and Eleanor, to do the same. But type As' propensity for doing and thinking many things simultaneously—while expecting the same from others—is a formula for alienation.

As type A relationships develop and evolve, our partner, as was the case with Eleanor, begins to feel weighed down by criticism. Amid the stress of being judged, they're likely to rebel, withdraw, become angry, or use whatever tactics they can to survive.

Our initial response is to notch up once again. So a circular pattern develops: The more the partner on the receiving end feels judged and criticized, the less cooperative he or she becomes and the more anxious the type A becomes, alienating the other partner further and preventing him or her from getting what he or she wants.

As the struggle to gain or maintain control deteriorates further, we eventually become less sensitive to our reactions and the effect they are having on our partner. Inevitably, we kill the comfortableness and closeness of our relationships and drift into a strange form of passivity that's accompanied by feelings of hopelessness and helplessness.

Unlike our usual response, especially in the workplace, we withdraw, operating separately from our spouses and families. This is an important reason why so many relationships flounder and why many couples end up living somewhat miserably thereafter.

Rather than learning to monitor how type A behavior plays out in relationships and developing new skills, the partner on the receiving end withdraws, and in time, the high-powered partner does the same. What happens is that a paralyzing contempt, rather than a growth-facilitating affection, becomes the predominant theme in the exec relationship.

Change Can Be a Friend

Mutual alienation begins with change. After all, what is the point of criticism, if not to get another person—in a totally ineffective manner—to change? It is one person saying to the other, "I don't like the way things [you] are; do it this way!"

Change need not be the enemy—it is the manner in which we approach it that will make or break our relationship. In a successful business venture *all* stakeholders must remain fluid and open to change. Indeed, a formidable barrier to growth and prosperity is an unwillingness to adapt to changing conditions. Not only is personal or professional change inevitable, it is also *necessary* as conditions change.

Look what happened at the Schwinn bicycle company. Rather than address the major mountain bike trend of the eighties and the high-end, lightweight bicycle competition coming from Europe, Schwinn kept to a marketing strategy that neglected the changing needs of cyclists. As a result, Schwinn, once a household name in bicycles, went bankrupt in 1992.

In like manner, the dominating barrier to marital satisfaction, or for that matter, to progress in any relationship—whether with colleagues, employees, friends, or family members—is resistance to change. *The great marital paradox is that people will only change if they don't feel they have to!*

The history of business is replete with efforts to overcome resistance and to influence others with every imaginable negative device ranging from punishment to devious flattery. These efforts have been outstanding failures; most of us resist, covertly or blatantly, the demand that we live up to others' visions of what we "should" be.

In relationships the rebellion may take many forms—overeating, lack of cooperation, substance abuse, infidelity, or, in more extreme instances, suicide. As we've seen with John and Eleanor, in its active state, resistance to imposed change may result in chronic arguing, withdrawal, or complete estrangement.

All of us strive to maintain our own identity as unique, independent persons. To frustrate this tendency is to ask for grief.

Bear in mind that negotiating the potholes that litter the path of most exec relationships leaves all couples stressed. Still, some find ways to cope with the pressures that accompany their hectic lives. As in every human endeavor, there are those who manage to get it right, despite facing the same circumstances that defeat others.

Consider Rob's take on being a stay-at-home dad (SAHD), an arrangement that seriously challenges the usual gender roles.

I became a[n] SAHD with the birth of my son three years ago, and despite my initial reservations, it's working. I am not advocating it for everyone. If I was super ambitious and felt I had a major contribution that was being stifled by our arrangement it wouldn't work. As it is, my wife is the one with the bursting ambition. That's cool with me. If we had met in the era before women had real career opportunities, we'd both be pretty unhappy. She'd be depressed and restless, and I would be working my ass off and missing time with my children. We would probably be taking out our grief on each other and making a mess of things. Instead, our courage to buck the conventional gender roles has allowed us to do what we really want in life.

Some of my friends were worried for me. "She'll run all over you, don't do it," was the refrain that a few of them echoed. It gave me some pause, but I didn't buy it. Men need not fear a loss of power when they become a[n] SAHD. Sure, I realize that most of the women who are eager to make the trade-off are the "high-testosterone," more dominant type As. SAHDs are stereotyped as being "pussy-whipped"; in reality, I have more power in the family now than I ever did when I was the breadwinner. I am in charge of the kids! Kitty is an equal partner in major decisions, but I supervise and have the day-to-day influence on the children. What could be better than that? The household revolves around me!

Rob and Kitty bucked the odds and created a successful relationship. I was impressed by the way they handled their unconventional role switch, so I sat down with them and four other successful SAHD couples and asked for the top tips they would give to other couples considering their arrangement—or those who have adopted this arrangement, but are not faring as well. Here's a compilation of what they said:

- **Appreciate the benefits.** With reduced familial responsibilities, women can compete more evenly with career-oriented men. For men, it is an opportunity to see your children grow up and to experience some of the activities our fathers never did, like seeing your son take his first steps.
- **Discard the have-it-all notion.** Rob, Kitty, and the others spoke of missing something at first, but they worked at reconciling themselves to that, appreciating the benefits rather than focusing on what they were giving up. For example, it took some effort on Kitty's part to accept the notion that Mom is not number one in her son's life. It also occurred to them that they might get locked into this arrangement. After Rob is off the career track for a few years, it will be harder to switch roles if Kitty wants to get out. This, Kitty explained, is one of the reasons many women prefer life as part of a frazzled two-earner couple. Keeping the man on the career track as the main breadwinner helps to preserve women's options.
- **Fend-off conventional thinking.** Rob and several of the other guys said that some of their friends still denigrate their choice and feel they are unmanly. As Rob put it, "It's as if the word 'wimp' is on the tip of their tongue[s]." Clearly, the SAHD will have to endure the unconscious hypocrisy of a society that often wrings its hands over the lot of the housewife, yet at the same time views SAHDs as freeloaders who have

left their working wives holding the bag. Just as women sometimes aren't taken seriously by men in the corporate boardroom, Rob and the other men also get a quizzical look from their children's teachers if they go to a daytime school meeting, as if to say, "Why aren't you at work?"

- **Deal with boredom creatively.** Many stay-at-home parents face boredom and social isolation, but it can be particularly acute for SAHDs, since there are few other men at home, and connections with stay-at-home moms can be difficult to cultivate. A couple of the men acknowledge that boredom and opportunity tempted them to have an affair. One did, but the other decided instead to use his online resources to create a "Dad and Me" group. As an added benefit, he made friends with a guy who has become his closest buddy.

Clearly, the SAHD arrangement is not for everyone. However, to their credit, Rob and Kitty and the other couples, while perhaps more suited for their roles, worked hard to overcome the obstacles.

Regardless of the arrangement, executive marriage is always a formidable challenge, especially since most exec marriages have one person, the more dominant type A, who has a tendency to control, and control rarely works over the long term.

To help you become one of the couples who gets it right, three principles that defend individuality and challenge unwanted coercion are addressed. Contrary to those fruitless attempts to bully our partners, the problem of how to control *ourselves* will be confronted.

Taken together, the three principles that follow offer a method for creating desired change by engaging rather than alienating.

Empower Yourself

The first is the principle of Individual Responsibility.

Each of us has the capacity to change. When we assign responsibility for our malaise to another person, we impede our change potential and render ourselves powerless.

A couple has a fight. The wife feels irritated with her husband because he did not call her during the four days he was traveling on business. They go to bed that evening without saying a word to each other. She is no longer angry and would like her husband to make contact with her—talk to her, reach out to her, caress her. He, not knowing that her mood has passed and fearing that she is still upset, does nothing of the sort, deciding to wait until she gives him some indication that she will respond to him more kindly. She is not willing to reach out and make contact herself, although she would like to do so. Lying there, she begins to blame him for not "making a move," for not doing something she herself is unwilling to do.

A husband, ironically a CFO, is a very poor manager of money. His debts pile up unpaid. His one major avenue to recovery is to file for a substantial federal income tax refund dating back several years. He procrastinates despite his wife's pleading. The bills continue to pile up, adding more pressure to the couple's tensions. Finally, the husband files for his refund and receives a prompt reply from the Internal Revenue Service stating that his request exceeded the cutoff date and was no longer valid. He immediately blames his wife, saying she should have "kept after him." When she grows angry and tells him that his failure to get things done is driving her to distraction, he continues to deny personal responsibility and takes the blame to a new level. "If it was that important to you," he says, "why didn't you lock me out of the house or something until I filed the return?"

In the above examples, the blamer has the attitude, "I'm not responsible, you are." From this follows, or is implied, "If you are responsible for my [our] discomfort, distress, or unhappiness, only you can alter it." In each of these instances the blamer is being dishonest in an effort to avoid responsibility for his or her behavior. What's more, there is an inherent assumption that the blamer is powerless and therefore at the mercy of the other partner. Unless the circumstance is very unusual, like being held at gunpoint, adults are rarely powerless.

The following statements, similar to those I spotted years ago in the classic book *The Mirages of Marriage* are characteristic of this powerless attitude:

> "If you would only make me feel welcome, I'd be home more of the time."
>
> "If you stopped going golfing so often and stayed home more, I wouldn't act so nasty."
>
> "If only you didn't drink so much, I wouldn't be so bitchy."
> "If you weren't so bitchy, I wouldn't drink so much."
>
> "If you encouraged me instead of condemning me, I would be more responsive."

"If you would only do things right, I would have the incentive to be encouraging."

"If you were only more informed and well read, I would have more to say to you."

"If only you paid attention to me and showed me that my opinion counted, I would feel more confident in expressing it."

"If only you'd stop pampering the children, I would become more involved in parenting."

"If only you'd become more involved with the children, I wouldn't have to be both mother and father to them."

"If you'd hold my hand and pay attention to me at parties, I wouldn't flirt."

"If you weren't such a flirt at parties, I wouldn't feel so alienated from you."

If it would help the relationship for the wife to be less flirtatious and the husband to be more attentive at parties, who is to take the initiative? And will the person making the first move be regarded by the spouse as having been wrong all along?

When couples relate in such a blame-oriented way, they create a major obstacle to relating. Nothing is resolved if both husband and wife are constantly screaming or silently sulking about who is to blame. *Resolution is unlikely unless one partner is willing to take on-the-spot initiative.* He or she must drop the passive role. Just as coercion divides, positive initiative unites.

Typically in the blame–counter-blame trap, both partners issue their complaints *after* the unwanted behavior has occurred but do nothing while it is taking place. A husband may accuse his wife of being inconsiderate because she repeatedly interrupts him. He will nag, complain, sulk, and admonish, but rarely will he take a firm stand while the behavior is actually happening. What if while being interrupted he stated, "You're interrupting me, Barbara. Please let me finish what I'm saying."

If this didn't work, he might simply get up and leave the room, saying, "It seems, by your constant interruptions, that you are not interested in what I'm saying. When you feel more like listening, let me know." Although this behavior may seem harsh, it works.

Jane harbors resentment toward Bill because he doesn't pay attention to her at social gatherings. Yet this behavior has continued on Bill's part for a long period of time, so it is likely that Jane has been blaming and antagonizing him rather than taking responsibility for getting what she wants: more attention.

Perhaps she goes off in a corner at parties to sulk or becomes nasty and sarcastic about Bill's social adroitness. Later, when they are alone, she may withdraw or explode and tell Bill his behavior makes her furious. Her comments will then elevate their conflict into a fight or mutual withdrawal.

If Jane would take responsibility for her shyness, envy of her husband's social popularity, or desire for more attention, rather than waiting for him to "save her," she would be approaching her issues more honestly, rather than hiding behind her complaints, and a major stumbling block to a functional relationship would be removed.

This might involve a total cessation of blame, working to overcome her social shyness, and making a concerted effort to be part of her husband's conversations instead of withdrawing from them and stewing. In fact, if she did nothing to work on her social shyness but simply declared it rather than blame her husband, she could break the cycle of mutual recrimination and restore opportunities for productive relating.

Positive Reframing

Closely related to the principle of personal empowerment is the principle of Reframing.

To reframe means to change one's viewpoint in relation to an event, to give a situation new meaning.

As the philosopher Epictetus expressed in the first century A.D., "People are disturbed not by things, but by the views which they take of them." Stated differently, we don't view things as they are, but as *we* are.

What governs behavior are our unique perceptions of ourselves and the world in which we live; the meanings we give to the events of our lives. This fact seems obvious enough, but in reality most of us do not appreciate the enormity of its application. Perhaps more than any other behavioral scientist, my former postdoctoral fellowship mentor, psychologist Albert Ellis, the most influential living psychologist and the father of cognitive-behavior therapy, has championed recognition of this principle.

Ellis refers to this idea as the "ABC theory of personality and emotional disturbance," and stresses that it is not the activating events (A) that cause emotional consequences (C), but rather the individual's beliefs (B) about what occurred at point A.

According to Ellis, most of us are drawn to mistaken beliefs with costly results, both in individual and interpersonal aspects of our lives. This may cause us to demand perfection, insist that life go smoothly, and dictate that people act with absolute fairness and kindness.

It is certainly a desirable wish that everyone, in all our dealings, be competent and that the world not present us with petty and not-so-petty frustrations, or that other people always be considerate. However, the *insistence* that things *must* be that way leads to emotional upset and self-defeating behavior. It is simply not how the world operates, although we execs sometimes act as though our sole purpose on earth is to institute reform.

Any number of examples may be cited to clarify the ABC philosophy, but let us take one typical occurrence as a case in point. A mid-level executive appears preoccupied much of the time and pays little attention to his partner (activating event). His partner decides that he has no regard for her feelings at all (belief system), so she becomes angry (consequence) and tears into him about his selfishness (another consequence). Now the woman blames her partner for *making* her angry. According to Ellis's approach, the woman's anger and outburst is under *her control, not her husband's*.

She could have viewed his behavior in several other ways, for example, "He may be worried about something" or "He really gets involved in his work" or "He has difficulty managing his time" or "He simply requires less companionship." Even if the husband were acting selfishly, what guarantee is there that he will behave desirably all the time? Accepting her husband's lesser need for companionship (which is equivalent to reasonable tolerance, not preference) or viewing his behavior in less inflammatory terms would have enabled this woman to react in a more effective manner.

The point here is this: All behavior is open to many interpretations, and the particular interpretation chosen directly influences the feelings and behavioral reactions that are generated. Discordant interaction arises when one mate views the other's behavior negatively (often in the worst possible manner) and *insists* that his or her perception is accurate and that the other partner change, all the while feeding into this downward spiral by reacting spitefully and demandingly. Then the other mate, by dwelling on the negative reaction ("That S.O.B. isn't going to get away with this"), continues his or her negative behavior, and an outburst of temper on the part of one or both spouses ensues. According to the principle of reframing, instead of feeling powerless and without control, we must accept responsibility for our own fate; it is *our* choice to make or to refuse to make ourselves seriously distressed. The effort to train ourselves to reframe—"How can I view this situation in the most productive (and realistic) manner possible?"—is likely to be rewarded by increased harmony and avoidance of unnecessary stress.

Since our individual interpretations of behavior are largely the product of experience, there is no more effective way of affecting or changing those interpretations than through introducing new kinds of experiences. It is rare that we are successful in changing perceptions either in ourselves or in others simply by will, unless this process is accompanied by some kind of experience as well.

Such change may be accomplished through open discussions with others in which beliefs can be explored and subjected to the influence of other personalities. Sometimes old perceptions can be re-examined in a more solitary fashion, as when we set ourselves the task of "thinking through" an idea. Occasionally, creative activities like painting or music or writing aid the process.

Perhaps the most important way in which individuals can arrive at a new understanding of behavior is through deliberately breaking away from the usual patterns, in other words, changing one's own behavior. Your behavior should be consistent with beliefs that are productive and positive, even if those beliefs are not yet convictions.

Overcoming Fear

Change requires flirting with inadequacy; having the courage to fumble and a willingness to open ourselves to a degree of current uneasiness in the hope that greater satisfaction will be derived in the long run. Something must be ventured if there is to be any gain.

This, of course, is not easy and brings us to the Fear-of-Change principle.

> *In most areas of our lives, we put a premium on security and resist change even if the novel behavior holds the promise of long-term gains.*

There are a number of obstacles to be overcome. First, particularly for type As, is the difficulty of letting ourselves go, rather than tightening the grip on our feelings. Many of us type As fear losing control. However, if you give expression to your feelings and resist the temptation to be defensive, you are less likely to lose control. In fact, the very fear of losing control usually results in denying feelings, which build up to trigger arguments and explosions.

Frequently, both spouses feel they have been victimized in the relationship, forced to give more than they have received. Both partners, as we have seen, typically decide to withhold positive changes on the basis of pride; they feel that "giving in" implies they have been wrong all along.

In essence, they adopt a "change second" rather than a "change first" attitude, which results in a hopeless deadlock. The change-second attitude translates to "I will change in response to your change." In contrast, the change-first attitude plays out as "Taking initiative is in my best interest."

Just as false pride makes progress more difficult, inertia also comes into play as well. This is the tendency for an established pattern to remain unaltered. In order for us to move forward, an extra push is often needed. Once the initial energy is exerted and change is well under way, less effort will be required. But we are often reluctant to exert this extra energy, and balking as well as rebellion is to be expected.

That vague (and sometimes not-so-vague) sense of losing control, though, has the most powerful effect on the change process. Fear is the feeling that engulfs us when we seriously consider altering a pattern that is well established, even if it is dysfunctional.

Edward Henley, a forty-five-year-old entrepreneur, knows this feeling well. Depressed for many months, out of desperation he followed his physician's advice and consulted me. Now, three months after a year-long therapy experience, he discusses his struggle to confront his fear.

> At first, the idea of psychological help seemed strange to me. I wondered, "How can this help me—just talking about things that aren't even clear to me?" But I found that talking, having to put my vague thoughts into words, forced me to think of things I hadn't considered in many years; it had the effect of making me dig deep inside myself and bring up things I hardly knew were troubling me. As we continued to meet, I spoke more easily of my relationship with my wife, Mary. In one conversation, I felt as if I had come to the edge of an awful canyon; I referred to it later as a pit I had dug for myself. I became aware that all these years were spent avoiding involvement with Mary. I really had no intimacy; after seventeen years of marriage, I wasn't close to her or to anyone else. If Mary was getting too close, I busied myself with work, limiting the amount of time I spent with

her; even if I revealed a personal feeling, I did so in a controlled manner, making sure not to be *too* revealing. Basically, I had this feeling that if Mary, or anyone else for that matter, really got to know me, I would be a total disappointment. I guess I don't have much value in myself as a person.

At one point in our conversation, I remarked that I haven't let myself really be loved by anyone. The statement was true and it was agonizing, but there was still a buffer between the words and my experience. It wasn't quite real; it didn't penetrate my armor. You asked me to repeat my statement slowly and as I did so to focus on my feelings. I did it once and I started to feel weak; I felt wobbly even though I was seated. You asked me to do it again, and I tried but I could barely speak. I felt more deeply disturbed than I can describe; I had reached a point far away from anything I had ever known. Despair, fear, and grief, all greater than I had felt before, were evoked by the thought of changing, increasing my vulnerability to hurt. Suddenly, I was engulfed in emotion beyond anything I had ever experienced.

As soon as our session ended, I went home and forced myself to sleep. I was scared and unhappy when I woke up. I couldn't rid myself of the thought that I had withdrawn from significant human contact; I was not even intimate with myself. I would not allow myself to experience my feelings about myself, and I managed to avoid the intensity of the previous conversation. I was angry and confused, afraid of what I felt and even more frightened of what I needed to do in order to change. I felt lost, and for the first time since childhood I felt real panic. I skipped several appointments with you in an effort to run away from what I was feeling, but I found those feelings impossible to deny. You encouraged me gently but persistently to risk being open, to let things happen to my feelings, and to expose them. Gradually, I was even able to reveal more of my "true self" to Mary.

Fear can be obvious and overpowering, as it was for Edward. In other instances, fear makes its appearance in a more subtle or deceptive manner: through excuses, bravado, lethargy, helplessness, rebellion, resentfulness, and the like. Whatever the form, fear is practically always a part of the change process, and its presence demands respect. Pushing too hard is likely to be met with more resistance. Lack of challenge, on the other hand, will encourage complacency.

All this may be discouraging, feeding the common and false belief that deep down people can't change or that a marriage cannot improve unless both partners change. The truth is that change is not only possible, it is inevitable. The challenge is to affect positive change. Positive change starts with you. Recognize that changing—giving more or giving something different to your spouse—doesn't make you *less*, it makes you *more* for having the courage to make things better.

Outline your reasons for initiating a change process. What do you like/dislike about the way things are in the relationship? What is driving the idea of change? You? Your goals? Your partner? What do you have to give up if you make this change? Before you seek to make a change, be clear what you want to stop doing, and what you want to do instead.

Tool Kit

The transformation required in order for a relationship to become rewarding is, of course, neither simple nor instant. There is not one dramatic issue to be repaired, but a series of little separations that, over time, like termites, have eaten away at the emotional connection. To avoid the pitfalls inherent in the change process, whether for yourself, or as a couple, here are several guidelines that have proven to be effective:

1. **Express feelings, not demands.** As we have seen, casting blame in love relationships does not work and is often dishonest. To avoid blame, consider beginning your statements with a form of the pronoun "I" ("Me," "my," "mine"). "I" statements are expressions of responsibility; beginning a sentence with "I" personalizes your feelings or thoughts. Note that tacking a prefix like "I think that you..." or "I feel that you..." onto a sentence does not make it an "I" statement. An "I" statement is a report of your awareness of yourself, not of the other person: "I resent being told what to do" rather than "You are too bossy."
2. **Be gradual.** A great many attempts at change fail because they are too sweeping in nature. Misguided attempts to change something about themselves or their relationships too quickly or too dramatically in too short a period of time are responsible for a good deal of the disillusion-

ment and despair many people feel. For example, when a woman is dissatisfied with her partner's lack of participation in household chores, she may request broad changes in his behavior that he is quite likely to resist, since the request for change will be perceived as overwhelming. However, if the requests are gradual and successively approximate the desired level of participation, the process of change is more likely to proceed more smoothly.

3. **Expect resistance.** Compounding the difficulty we all have with the change process is that change in relationships often involves taking the risk of moving closer to another person. While we want the rewards of closeness, many of us fear the increased vulnerability and the possibility of being hurt that accompanies intimacy. To counter resistance in another person be a model for what you want. Do you want more warmth, for example? If so, are you giving what you want to get?

4. **Be persistent.** Both parties can be expected to test the sincerity of each other's change efforts. Testing may take the form of questioning motivation ("You're doing this only because you're afraid I'll leave you"); or attempting to discount the change effort ("These changes are just too artificial and trivial"); and/or a return to earlier, relationship-defeating behaviors. By viewing testing as a natural part of the change process and continuing with the novel behavior pattern despite temporary discouragement, a new precedent is set.

5. **Be positive.** It is much easier to increase positive behavior than it is to directly eliminate negative behavior. For example, rather than emphasizing a suppression of excessive criticism, a spouse is likelier to be effective if he or she concentrated on a response incompatible to criticism—an increase in positive, appreciative comments. Behavioral science research suggests that undesirable behaviors are more effectively controlled when confronted in this positively oriented manner.

6. **Be behavioral.** Although feelings and beliefs are critically important in a relationship, neither carries the impact of action. Telling a partner you love them does not have the immediacy and potency of a demonstration. Relationship change, therefore, is founded on paying close attention to what you do—"Am I behaving in a manner that promotes relationship satisfaction?"—rather than simply what you profess.

Discussion Forum

Go back to John and Eleanor, the couple whose story opened this chapter. John has a point, as does Eleanor. Reverse each partner's position (the husband takes Eleanor's, the wife takes John's) and make each case, fleshing out their concerns, digging into the feelings underlying their complaints. This will give you practice with understanding another person's perspective. Then, come up with one of your own concerns and, applying the guidelines above, develop a plan to change something in the relationship that both of you agree would be of mutual benefit.

I better change direction or I am going to get where I'm going—and it's not where I want to be!

STRATEGY THREE

Develop a Culture of Collaboration

Active Caring

In marriages like ours there are discouraging periods where we may believe we are destined to fail. While many do fail, a significant percentage of couples are able to keep their romance alive. They do so in a manner that's graceful, flexible, and obviously effective, while maintaining high levels of passion and emotional closeness.

From the way they whisper to one another, still hold hands, and flirt, it's clear they care deeply. They're living testaments that an intimate relationship is not incompatible with a dynamic career. And they remind us of an important lesson: Stress is inevitable; struggling is optional.

Consider the story of Lisa Daniels. She is the CEO of a textile firm that grosses nearly a half billion dollars a year. She would never think of vacationing without her husband, a physician. She spends most nights in his company, and unlike many of her high-powered peers she has managed to avoid the workaholic trap. I very much wanted to hear her secrets.

When I met Lisa I was not disappointed. Not only does she juggle many roles, she seems to relish every moment. I couldn't help wondering: Does she embody Donna Reed? Wonder Woman? A Stepford wife? Actually, none of the above.

In Lisa's mind, it is possible to have it all—well, not all, but almost, and the "almost" is important. Unrealistic expectations, in Lisa's view, is where a part of the problem many couples face lies. She doesn't waste time on things that are not important to her or her husband, Michael, and she has her eye on her priorities. While I was speaking to her and Michael, it was apparent that they were stars in the dual-income couple challenge.

"Do you have tips for other two-income executive couples?" I asked. Not only was Lisa happy to discuss this, she brought three other couples to our discussion, all of whom were in dual-income marriages with high-responsibility careers. Here's what they had to say:

- **Give your needs priority.** For example, early in her career, Lisa would work late with the proviso that her boss conceded to her leaving early on important family occasions. She has also become skilled at negotiating the sharing of household and parenting chores with her husband. Yes, she allowed, she does more, but the (uneven) distribution works for her—as it did for the other couples.
- **Maintain family time.** All of the couples were aware of the need for family time and, consequently, were very selective with unnecessary meetings and tasks. "Michael has a hospital practice and there are lots of events he is asked to attend," Lisa said. "I also have a lot of extracurricular demands on my time. We only go to those events that are necessary; our family life does not even permit those that are desirable but unnecessary—and we don't bow to PC in having to both show up to all events."
- **Access resources.** "There was a time I felt I had to do everything myself, the way my mother did," one of the other women offered. "But there are lots of things that neither of us want to do, nor have the time for—whether a minor repair or making the bed. Either we leave it undone, or have someone else do it. As for our relationship, we also bring in specialists. We go to enhancement workshops twice a year for a tune-up."
- **Become a change master.** All of these successful couples recognize that changes will occur, whether in their career or family life, and intentionally gain the skills needed to achieve success in the new direction. For example, one couple stated that when their son was diagnosed with some neurological problems, both parents were trained by the occupational therapist so that they could share in administering his treatment.
- **Make family-promoting decisions.** If work and family are on a collision course, choose family. All of the couples make decisions in favor of their family life. For example, one couple spoke of one partner's not taking a lucrative position that required a significant

relocation and loss of opportunity for the other, or a position that was tempting but was quite apparently over-the-top demanding.

There was one other issue I wanted to hear more about from the group. "Are there any particular tips for avoiding the workaholic trap?" I asked them before they departed.

They agreed with my contention that the emotional pain caused by workaholism, a popular term for the compulsive drive to work above all else, must be addressed to avoid irreparable damage. It has been my experience that workaholics have a compulsive need for the approval and power that come with achievement. Over time, they lose touch with their emotions. Indeed, divorce is a common outcome according to Workaholics Anonymous, a self-help group with thirty-two U.S. chapters.

Getting around the workaholic's ironclad defenses, such as "I'm doing this because I care about you," is no small task. I found that even in this well-functioning group, several of the spouses were recovering workaholics. From their own experience, they suggested that in addition to the tips above, it was crucial to avoid a power struggle with a workaholic, rather, focus on expressing your unmet needs and negotiating a way to meet them.

One woman noted that her anger sometimes led her to criticize her husband's work habits. But she found that pushed him away, the opposite of what she wanted. She learned to take a breather when she was upset, and when she had calmed down she negotiated for changes. Each couple favored short breaks, such as stepping away from the computer for a few minutes, or taking a family walk in the neighborhood. "Even short time-outs help prevent a downward spiral of loneliness," one of the men in the group said.

While these tips are particularly valuable for exec marriages, especially those that are challenged by two working partners, in one sense, there is no difference between exec marriages and any other.

Executive marriages go through the same phases all long-term relationships go through, only faster: high levels of emotional closeness for about two years; an abrupt drop-off in intimacy, due to increased responsibilities, babies, and mortgages after year five; and finally, a diminishing of tenderness and affection when our needs begin to collide with the stresses of our lifestyle.

In this last phase, exec couples may stay together, but our relationships get stale. We're often less thoughtful of each other. The little things that were present and frequent in the first two years have dropped out. The ratio of positive to negative statements has become unfavorable.

Relationships, like business ventures, prosper or fail on little things, things that wouldn't make a good movie, like saying "please" and "thank you," laughing at each other's jokes, touching, and being there for each other.

Why is it so many exec relationships become stagnant, while other exec couples create alliances that are highly caring, loving, and warm? The answer is available to anyone who wants to acknowledge it: Those relationships that are vibrant continue to exhibit more positive behaviors of the sort that were evident in the early years, the years when love was a verb.

Here's the skinny: The balance between negative and positive appears to be the key dynamic in the emotional foundation of every marriage. There seems to be some kind of thermostat operating in healthy marriages that regulates this balance. For example, when partners get contemptuous, they correct it with lots of healing gestures—not necessarily right away, but sometime soon after the conflict.

What really separates contented couples from those in deep marital misery is that contented couples have achieved a healthy balance between their positive and negative feelings and actions toward each other. Research confirms this: a study compared divorced and married couples with the assumption that they would find that the divorced couples had more problems. That wasn't the case. All the couples had problems. The difference was the far greater number of positive statements the married couples made to each other. The exact ratio? Three to one in favor of positives!

The parallel in business is illustrated by a small group of account managers at RCA who increased the size of their accounts each year by tens of millions of dollars in sales. How? It wasn't because they were smarter or more tech savvy than other sales managers. It was because they actively created and nurtured their business relationships. They realized that relationship-building was key and made sure that positive statements and actions were traded among them and their clients.

It comes down to this: A healthy relationship requires *active* concern on the part of each individual for the satisfaction and growth of the other. It's about creating a culture of collaboration, such as was created by a group of superstar computer programmers whose rate of producing successful programs was a startling 1,272 percent more than the average. "It's not just computing skills that set them apart, but teamwork," contends Lyle Spencer, Jr., director of the research firm that discussed their success at an international conference. "The very best don't compete, they collaborate."

Active collaboration in your marriage means that the concerned person *acts*. He or she engages in behavior aimed at providing satisfaction and growth in the other. Those behaviors, viewed as supportive and collaborative expressions, may vary from person to person.

One woman, a forty-four-year-old artist, married for twenty years to the CFO of an international data systems firm, expressed her views to me in this way.

> Caring doesn't mean rushing into action at every crisis and making it all better. When a child falls and hurts herself, the mother who "cares" too much glosses over the pain by mouthing words that are empty and unrealistic: "There now, don't cry, that doesn't hurt." What the child wants, though, is for her mother to understand how she really feels: "There now, of course it hurts, no wonder you are crying. Soon it will mend and you will feel better."
>
> For me, caring in an adult relationship is the same thing. If the quality of my work is disappointing, for example, I don't want someone to simply rationalize for me or entertain me into a frozen smile; someone who cares doesn't deny my feelings. I want, instead, someone who will listen carefully and try to understand. My husband doesn't do that; he is so caught up in his business that he simply dismisses my concerns out of hand: 'Oh, don't worry, things will work out.' I feel as if I hardly exist in his life. I've adjusted to that, but it saddens me and limits the relationship. More of my emotional investment is directed toward my women friends; they lend a sympathetic ear. It is with them that I really feel nurtured.

Collaboration, the feeling that you have a teammate who cares about you, is a much sought-after goal in a relationship. In a sense, the actively caring person can be thought of as a "supply source" of satisfaction; most of us are drawn to "suppliers," people who act positively toward us. In this atmosphere we feel valued. No doubt, demonstrated caring is a very powerful relationship asset.

Once again, the payoff in business is nothing less than spectacular. In another study reported by Spencer and his firm, this time of salespeople in forty-four Fortune 500 firms, including AT&T, IBM, and PepsiCo, those who were committed to a collaborative approach—being positive and supportive with colleagues and their market—performed at a level that was more than twice the average.

The same applies in relationships. Research evidence and clinical experience suggest that people tend to be more strongly attracted to others who behave toward them in a caring manner. In fact, positive actions are likely to promote positive reactions, first in the attitudes of others, then in their behavior.

When an intimate partner demonstrates support and collaboration, we feel liked and in turn deepen our liking for this person. Thus, we acquire a vested interest in the satisfaction of an intimate, and by so doing we increase the likelihood of achieving our own satisfaction.

It makes compelling sense: A satisfied partner is better able and more willing to provide for another's satisfactions than a dissatisfied partner.

Caring, Long Distance

What about being responsive and connected when one spouse travels extensively? Here, the challenge of maintaining marital satisfaction requires innovation.

Marion, a woman married fifteen years to Foster, who travels extensively in his role as director of marketing for a graphics equipment company, described her experience to me.

> When we were first married, I accompanied Foster on his trips to the Middle East three or four times. The trips certainly were not fun; they were exhausting and often boring. I spent most of the time alone in a hotel room while Foster tended to business. So I stopped going, and our contact was minimal and strained for long periods of time. Occasionally, we would write brief notes or phone, but only occasionally. I felt like a fixture in Foster's life and greeted him with a growl when he finally arrived home. Those were difficult days. When we were both just a slight push from the divorce lawyer's office, we sat down and had a very serious, thoughtful conversation. It wasn't feasible for Foster to change jobs, nor was it any longer very practical for me to accompany him—what would I do with two children? We talked about other ways to bridge the gap, to keep our feelings for each other alive.

Now when Foster's away, he is more thoughtful of me. He phones several times a week. We e-mail and both write long letters that are intimate and detailed. Those letters, either on email or sometimes FedExed, reinforce our feelings for each other. Of course, I get lonely while Foster's away. But I plan ahead. I purchase theater and concert tickets; I let our friends know I'm available for dinner invitations. I do these things because it is better than stewing. I feel better about myself, I no longer feel neglected or sorry for myself and, consequently, my attitude toward Foster is more positive when he returns. What's more, I spend a lot of time thinking about the relationship, our life together, planning shared time when he gets home. Foster does the same. When he comes home, we have all that to explore together.

Despite the span of thousands of miles and long periods apart, Marion and Foster were able to maintain their basis for intimacy. By demonstrating their caring for each other, they stayed involved, even under difficult circumstances.

Here, a summary of suggestions they provided for staying involved when traveling:

- **Phone.** Get an international card for your cell phone.
- **Email.** If heavy travel is part of your lifestyle, get tech savvy.
- **Write letters before you leave.** This can be especially connective if they are supportive, substantive, and personal, and there is one to be opened for each day you are away.
- **Keep a brief journal of the travel time.** Your stay-at-home partner can feel part of the trip when you return.
- **Take a full day immediately on return.** Make it exclusively for family and plan special time for your partner.

In addition to the above, an increasing number of executives are squeezing family time into their travels by taking their spouse along. It is one way to combine family time and maybe even a little recreation into jam-packed schedules, but it can also backfire if the couple does not strike the right balance between business and pleasure.

In a *New York Times* article (June 15, 2004), Francine Parnes reports on the findings of a poll published in the *2004 National Business Travel Monitor*. According to the poll, 60 percent of business travelers took their spouse on a business trip at least once in 2003 (15 percent said they took the children as well). Fifty percent said they were very likely to do so in the next two years. In response to another question, 68 percent said they had combined business trips with leisure trips at least once last year, up from 57 percent in 2002. Most companies allow employees to take their spouses on business trips as long as the employee picks up any extra cost.

Good idea? The arrangement usually works pretty well, but it can create marital tensions and, in extreme cases, damage an executive's career. Ms. Parnes interviewed a psychologist who recalled the case of a patient who was a rising star at his company until he attended a corporate retreat with his boss to which both men brought their wives.

The two women spent their days together and before long they were having intimate discussions about their marriages. The wife of the rising star exec despised how the boss treated his wife. She wasn't hesitant in pointing this out to her new friend. Six months later, the boss's wife, who continued to have contact with the subordinate's wife, filed for divorce, ending her 15-year marriage. And six months after that, sensing his boss's quiet rage, the subordinate found another job.

That's a nightmare. More often, though, a spouse's presence enriches business trips, especially if the couple makes a habit of traveling together. Since about 1997, Ms. Parnes reports in her article, an exec on the west coast who flies approximately 100,000 business miles a year has taken his wife on every trip except two—and not just for companionship.

"I outsource to her all the travel logistics," he said. "I can concentrate on meetings and be more efficient. Coming back to a hotel room, when you're done working all day and you can be with your spouse, brings a bit of home with you."

That's an excellent method of closing the gap in what could be a long-distance relationship. But here is where Ms. Parnes's report gets gritty. As all us grownups are aware, not every business traveler craves a bit of home. Ms. Parnes spoke with the chief executive of a travel agency who notes that some married executives travel with their girlfriends, and sometimes an executive will fit both the wife and the girlfriend into the same trip, he said. The wife accompanies her husband for the first few days of a trip and then flies home, and the girlfriend arrives the same afternoon.

I have seen this as well in my practice. A chief executive I was treating sometimes traveled with his wife and sometimes traveled and shared a room with one of his senior employees, a woman fifteen years younger than his wife. Everyone in the office was uncomfortable with this, no one knew what to do, and no one dared to say anything.

It was like one of those family secrets that wreaks havoc with morale and diminishes respect, especially when the participant is in a leadership position. In this instance, the chief was forced to have his mistress resign.

Those are the dramatic stories. More commonly, as Ms. Parnes aptly proposes in her article, things can go wrong not due to dalliance or a conspiracy of spouses, but to unanticipated business duties that can disappoint the spouse who tagged along and leave the other guilt-ridden. It is certainly not usual for plans to be overwhelmed by unexpected meetings, demanding clients, and the everyday issues that take up more time than anticipated.

Is it better to take your partner along, or not? One woman, a partner in an executive-search firm who was interviewed for the *New York Times* article, travels around 75,000 miles a year, and never takes her husband, a private investor. "You can't take a third wheel along and leave him to fend for himself without feeling guilty," she said. "We were at this gorgeous resort in Coral Gables, but while I was at meetings, he stayed in the room all day until the market closed and watched CNBC with the curtains drawn.

"If your attention is divided," she added, "you end up shorting both your business partner and your marital partner. It's like having a two-year-old pulling on you when you're trying to have a telephone conversation."

Once again, is it wise to combine business travel and marriage? First, I recommend that it be the decision of both partners, rather than a unilateral one. If your schedule appears as if it will be busy, and your partner is open to filling his or her time while you are occupied, it can be better than not having contact at all, especially if your travel schedule is heavy. In short, if expectations are realistic and aligned, and your spouse is desirous of accompanying you, it makes sense.

Romance Is Not Enough

Traveling is one thing, but making the most of the time at home is ultimately most important. Frequently, execs are so preoccupied with their work life that opportunities for small but important collaborative gestures are overlooked. They are lured into mistakenly believing that a post-honeymoon relationship moves along on its own energy and consequently do not bother to fuel it. It may work, but only temporarily. The marriage may survive for a couple of years on the initial romantic chemistry, but not much more.

It is especially important in the exec marriage *not* to rely on the absolute power of romance. Romance is like a fragile plant that, if not watered daily, begins to wilt. Exec marriages in particular need a strong dose of reality; they require a powerful yet efficient antidote to counter their unique lifestyle stressors.

Staying ahead of the curve is particularly important for a marriage expected to endure despite challenging conditions. If the relationship has begun to wilt, some couples become so imbedded in conflict that it never occurs to them to begin their repair process with small, manageable, positive actions. Even though a base hit is what is needed, execs think they have to aim for the fence and often strike out.

While some execs are aiming too high and missing opportunities, other couples attempt to demonstrate their concern for each other in a manner that is off the mark. "I don't think my husband loves me anymore. He certainly doesn't show it if he does," Susan commented to me about her husband, Gary.

She and Gary have been married ten years. Both are in demanding high-level positions in the cosmetics industry, and each feels increasingly neglected by the other.

Gary expresses his caring in practical, "sensible" ways. Instead of bringing flowers, which aren't practical, he brings home new kitchen gadgets; rather than phoning from the office, he works straight through and often quite late, hoping to earn a promotion. To Gary these are supportive expressions.

Although just as dedicated to her responsible position, Susan doesn't enjoy time in the kitchen and is opposed to making more money at the expense of family life. Consequently, Gary's misdirected efforts go unappreciated. But Susan is no better. Being sentimental and less practical, she will buy Gary a pair of furry slippers because they look so inviting and warm. She is put off by Gary's annoyance with these gifts. "It's a waste," he complains. "My feet sweat in these things. Besides, I don't like slippers, especially girly slippers!"

This may be one situation where the Golden Rule—do unto others as you would have others do unto you—is not the right approach. Spouse A believes that he is behaving in a loving, benevolent manner toward Spouse B. In reality, A is behaving in an insensitive, even selfish, manner ("If it pleases me, it should please you"). If B describes A's behavior as neglectful rather than caring, A is hurt and replies, "I was only trying to be loving."

George is an excellent cook. He does the shopping and prepares elaborate and rich meals regularly, which he regards as his way of expressing his love for Diane. Diane, however, is getting fatter by the month, her blood pressure is skyrocketing, and she is unhappy with herself. Diane tries to diet, but George makes it more difficult when he puts a hurt look on his face and explains how he spent the entire morning preparing that chocolate mousse she is refusing.

Is George's behavior simply misguided benevolence? Actually, George seems to be nurturing his own ego, upstaging Diane with his fancy preparations, encouraging her to feel less attractive. His "caring" behavior is more likely a form of one-upmanship, selfishness, and lack of consideration, behavior all humans are capable of at times. The point is that considering this behavior loving is self-deception.

There are many other examples of behavior that appear to be caring but are really selfish, or "pseudo-benevolent." Consider, for instance, the spouse who is greeted effusively at the door upon his return home from work. His partner insists on fussing over him and relaxing him with a drink (he abhors the taste of alcohol) despite his insistence that he relaxes best by having a few moments of solitude.

Or the husband who picks out an expensive gift—a new car, for instance—without first consulting with his wife. Often, the surprised recipient of such a purchase would have wanted to at least be given the option of choosing the model and accessories *she* wanted.

Then there's the protective partner who irritates under the guise of caring by constantly asking, "Are you all right?" "Is everything Okay?" Very brief separations are infused with telephone calls, emails, and inane small talk, all of which drives the recipient to distraction.

Keeping in Touch

One way to demonstrate caring is by reaching out and touching each other. Touch is a powerful collaboration-enhancing behavior. There is a hunger for body contact within all of us; tactile stimulation in the form of caressing, fondling, cuddling, embracing, stroking, and the like is a crucial relationship resource. Although touch itself is not an emotion, touching and being touched are often experienced emotionally.

In his wonderful book *Touching,* the late anthropologist Ashley Montagu suggests consulting a dictionary for the various meanings of the word "touch" to provide clues to the importance of this sensory experience. It is, for example, far and away the longest entry—fourteen full columns—in the authoritative *Oxford English Dictionary.*

Despite the desirability, and perhaps because of the potency of touching, it is often neglected in relationships. It seems that in this age of computers, cell phones, Blackberries and impersonal contact, combined with the PC and realistic sexual harassment concerns in the office, too many of us have become programmed to avoid touching or to confine it to a few permissible circumstances such as sex, athletics, casual greetings, and aggressive expressions.

This is highlighted by the results of an experiment conducted some years ago by Professor Kenneth Gergen and his colleagues in the Department of Psychology at Swarthmore College.

These researchers found that when persons were introduced into a pitch-black room in which there were half a dozen strangers, people they knew they would never meet again, more than 90 percent touched each other on purpose and nearly 50 percent hugged each other. In contrast, almost none of the participants in a similar group made any sort of tactile contact in a lighted room.

The researchers were struck by the desire of their darkroom subjects to make contact. Given anonymity, a group of perfect strangers moved very rapidly (it took about thirty minutes) to a stage of intimacy seldom attained in years of casual socializing. It was concluded from these findings that people share strong yearnings to be close to each other, but that our social norms discourage us from expressing these feelings physically: "Don't touch him [her]; he [she] may get the wrong idea."

Surprisingly, the idea that tactile stimulation is desirable, even necessary, for well-being has gained recognition only in recent years. When the results of psychologist Harry F. Harlow's ground-breaking experiments on infant monkeys were published, the subject of touching—especially the warm comfort of a mother's touch—came under close scientific scrutiny.

Briefly, what Harlow did was supply newborn monkeys with two artificial surrogate mothers, one warmed with a light bulb and covered with a soft terry cloth, the other merely a bare wire frame. The monkeys were divided into two groups, one given a nursing cloth mother, the other given a nursing wire-frame mother.

Dr. Harlow observed that the monkeys fed from the wire-framed mothers spent only enough time on those wire frames to stay alive. The rest of the time they spent clinging to the comforting cloth-covered mothers. Harlow wrote of the experiment: "We were not surprised to discover that contact comfort was an important basic affection or love variable, but we did not expect it to overshadow so completely the variable of nursing."

In essence, Harlow found that his infant monkeys valued tactile stimulation more than they did nourishment, for they preferred to cling to "mothers" who provided physical contact without nourishment to wire ones who did supply nourishment. Moreover, and perhaps most important, with deprived tactile stimulation, monkeys became nervous, awkward, irritable, and seriously impaired in their development.

There is little doubt that Harlow's findings have important implications for human beings. In adults, the need to be held, touched, and cuddled, like other needs, varies in intensity from person to person and, in the same person, from time to time, but it is present in all of us—and is especially crucial in our marital relationships.

Dr. Marc H. Hollender of the Vanderbilt School of Medicine has studied women and their reactions to touch. From their research, Hollender and his co-workers believe that for some women the need to be held or cuddled is a major determinant of sexual behavior.

In-depth interviews revealed that many women engage in sex with men when their real desire is to be held. As Hollender and his colleagues stated in the journal *Medical Aspects of Human Sexuality,*

> The desire to be cuddled and held is acceptable to most people as long as it is regarded as a component of adult sexuality. This wish to be cuddled and held in a maternal manner is felt to be too childish; to avoid embarrassment or shame, women convert it into the longing to be held by a man as part of an adult activity, sexual intercourse.

In another study, Hollender and an associate found that in the majority of women studied, there was a distinct increase in the desire to be held during pregnancy. This was assumed to coincide with the desire for demonstrated reassurance. In some women, those who felt themselves to be physically unattractive, there was a decrease in the frequency of requests to be held.

Such women, the investigators suggested, may have had a difficult time accepting physical affection because they felt unworthy, a consequence of their "poor" appearance. It may be interpreted by these findings that women are very much attuned to and desirous of touch, particularly during periods of vulnerability. Words are certainly important, but acts of touching that communicate affection and involvement are crucial.

Europeans have hugged and kissed each other for centuries. American men, in contrast, choose the more reserved handshake, the rugged slap on the back, or the poke in the ribs. Athletics are one of the few areas where men have permitted each other to touch and be touched through the rituals of swats across the behind and bear hugs, without fearing that their image would be tainted by demonstrations of "unmanly" behavior. Indeed, in athletic settings, football, for instance, the sporting activity is considered so masculine that all doubt is cancelled. It is like saying, in effect, "I've got masculinity to spare. I am very sure of myself."

Just as physical affection between men is masked by athletics or alcohol (picture the familiar scene of two drunks holding each other up), it is similarly disguised when relating to women. Here, sex becomes the major vehicle once again; hence the familiar lament of many women, "He touches me only when he wants sex."

Certainly, it would not be risky to venture that men as well as women long to be held and caressed without having to be sexually involved. It is apparent to most observers, though, that men have an even more difficult time than women acknowledging and satisfying their hunger for touch.

From Hercules to James Bond, the heroic man has been presented as impenetrable, unyielding, completely self-sufficient. Witness some discriminating reactions to male and female children: A shy little girl is considered cute; a shy boy is thought of as a sissy. A frightened girl is comforted; a boy is admonished to act like a man. Girls are allowed comfortably to kiss each other and to cry openly without shame; boys who even touch each other had better be horsing around, and crying is done only at the risk of incurring ridicule.

These behavioral distinctions were confirmed in a study that revealed that the majority of surveyed parents did not hug or cuddle their sons after the average age of five, would not kiss male children at all after a certain age, usually the onset of adolescence, and would discourage boys as young as four years old from sobbing by calling them crybabies or telling them to act their age.

When asked to explain the lack of physical affection and the prohibition against crying, the most common response from parents was, "I don't want my son to grow up to be a sissy."

It is apparent that from the moment of birth, touch is fundamental to the development of human behavior. Moreover, couples who minimize physical contact—exclusive of sexuality—are in danger of losing touch with each other. Besides the pleasures and satisfactions that come from the feel of a loved one's skin, touching provides an emotional link between intimates.

A compassionate touch can calm anxiety, ease pain, soothe fear, provide emotional security, and enhance collaboration, the "we're a team," feeling that is essential for marriages like ours. Yet our society, influenced as it has been by puritanical traditions, tends to discourage reaching out and touching one another.

Many of our inhibitions to touch are based on a concern with image, with how the touching will look to somebody else. Men are particularly plagued by this image problem; women are too, even if to a lesser extent. It may well be that after ignoring our desire for tactile contact, we are left with a vague sense of dissatisfaction—feeling isolated—but we no longer recognize its source.

Touch hunger, as with prolonged hunger for food, will eventually evaporate if not fulfilled. This does not mean that the requirement is gone, only that the pump must be primed in order to literally bring us to our senses.

Tool Kit

There is a host of ways to create collaboration, including, but not limited to, supportive touch.

Consider another example from the business world reported by Daniel Goleman in *Working with Emotional Intelligence*. Patrick McCarthy is a salesman in men's clothing at Nordstrom's flagship store in Seattle. Donald Peterson, the retired chairman of Ford Motor Company, is looking for a sports coat and he is a difficult fit. There is nothing in stock that is suitable.

A few days later, after tracking the request with one of his suppliers, McCarthy calls Peterson and tells him the jacket is on its way to him. This is typical behavior for McCarthy—he even phones the family of customers with gift suggestions when the customer has an upcoming occasion. What difference does McCarthy's customized service make? His annual sales are over $1 million in an industry where the average is around $80,000!

McCarthy's strategy strongly suggests that the best approach is an individually tailored program that infuses his relationship with his customers with a renewed atmosphere of goodwill and collaboration. Similarly, the best chance you have to feel loved, and have your partner feel the same way, is to have a clear idea of what makes each of you feel that way.

An effective and time-efficient method is the Mutual Support program. To begin, each partner is to ask the other, What would you like me to do as a means of giving you support and showing my concern for you? Answers to this question are assembled in a combined list, which will be conspicuously posted. After questioning your spouse about *behaviors* (not feelings or attitude) he or she considers supportive and collaborative, combine the list into one large chart. There are four criteria that a support request must meet before qualifying for listing.

1. **The request must be specific and positive.** "Make good eye contact when we speak" is positive; "stop looking at the floor when we speak" is negative. "Offer suggestions about my work problems" is specific; "Show me more consideration" is vague.
2. **The request must not be the focus of a recent conflict.** If frequency of sex is a burning issue, for instance, delay this agenda for the conflict-resolution procedures that we will discuss later.
3. **The behaviors must be of a type that can be performed at least once daily.** "Remembering special occasions" doesn't qualify; "Kissing good night" does.
4. **The behaviors must be small, minor acts, those that can be easily performed.** Do not include something that requires your partner to have a personality overhaul in order to accomplish it. If your partner is generally talkative, for instance, don't request long periods of silence.

Experience suggests that at least sixteen entries should be listed so that there is enough variation to allow each partner to sample a *minimum of two items daily*. If your list comes up short, it may be helpful to recall some of the pleasing behaviors exchanged during the beginning phase of your relationship, those you practiced during happy times, and add them to the chart.

If some of the listed behaviors appear unimportant or even trivial, don't be discouraged. Small gestures set the tone of a relationship, especially one that has been neglected, and can always be notched up at a later date.

Here's a sample list that Susan and Gary assembled after our discussion.

   Offer a cheerful greeting when either of us arrives home
   Compliment more (appearance, meals, parenting, etc.)

Call during the day just to say hello
Initiate conversation about the day's activities
Give a "mini" massage
Leave a love note
Make coffee in A.M.
Take out garbage
Help children with their homework
Make good eye contact when we speak
Make activity suggestions for an evening out
Offer suggestions about my work problems
Offer help with a chore
Discuss my interests with me
Express affection (holding hands, kissing, etc.)
Kiss good night
Wash my back when I'm in the shower
Touch me in a nonsexual but intimate manner

You can set up the list in a manner that allows for simple record keeping in the form of a check mark or perhaps even writing the date next to a behavior that occurred. In addition to performing the requested behaviors, it is helpful to have accurate information about how many desirable behaviors have been generated within the relationship during the course of time.

This written record helps each partner identify behaviors he or she may have overlooked, and by each partner recording the other's actions, it provides an acknowledgment and encouragement of positive behavior. As the checks or dates are filled in by the receiving spouse, the chart serves as a visual reminder of the collaborative atmosphere being developed.

Important supplements to the Mutual Support program follow:

1. **If you have children, you may want to include them in the program toward the end of the first week.** Explain your attempt to strengthen your teamwork with each other and patiently expand the chart to accommodate your children's participation. The Mutual Support chart is a living document that is subject to review and revision at any time. Eliminate behaviors as they become outdated; add others as they are requested.
2. **Each participant is to continue the collaborative expressions ir-**

respective of whether or not the other participants are continuing to make similar gestures.** It is not uncommon for one partner to test the other's commitment by unilaterally withdrawing. Gently put aside the excuses offered—"It's silly and artificial," "I don't have time," "This won't help"—and encourage commitment to the program.
3. **At the end of each week, each participant is to leave a brief note for the other participants acknowledging at least one caring gesture.** This is a reinforcing gesture that works well on the job and equally well at home. After all, how many of us wouldn't appreciate the chance to bathe in recognition for a job well done?

Sometimes a straightforward approach such as the Mutual Support program sounds good on paper, but exec couples that have neglected the relationship are often discouraged and, consequently, not motivated to participate. As one woman married to a man who practically considered her as part of the furniture asked me, "If I think and feel negatively, how am I going to behave collaboratively?"

It is here that a very powerful strategy, the As-If principle, described by the German philosopher Hans Vaihinger in 1877, comes into play. The As-If principle is based on the notion that changing our beliefs about a person (including ourselves) is most effectively accomplished by acting *as if* the change had already been achieved. Noted psychologist George Kelly, among others, reported great success with this approach. Dr. Kelly encouraged his clients to act as if they did not have the problem that distressed them. The shy college student, for example, was instructed to act as if he were self-assured when he approached girls on campus, and the critical husband was asked to act toward his wife as if her behavior were acceptable.

Assuming that the skills are available and the emotion (e.g., hurt, anger, and the like) is not unusually intense, acting *as if* creates an opportunity to go beyond the past, to dispel old prejudices through reality testing. Even a bumbling effort, if viewed liberally as a move in the right direction, initiates a new vision and provides a glimmer of what could be.

This same principle is fundamental to all relationship-building efforts. Commonly, for example, distressed partners complain of having "lost their feelings of love." Not feeling loving, they do not act loving. Herein lies the stalemate: Feelings of love will not magically appear; they can only be renewed through loving interaction with a partner. Therefore, the key to revitalizing the relationship is to act as if you feel loving, for only then do you increase the probability of stimulating your feelings of love as well as those of your partner. *Love is an effect of loving behavior.*

In brief, the sequence is to do something in order to feel something rather than to wait to feel something in order to do something. Every time you do something, the feelings and ideas consistent with that behavior are reinforced. It's as though the act recharges the feelings and beliefs that coincide with it. If you dislike someone, for example, disparaging him and trying to hurt him will increase your feelings of dislike.

If you want to increase your acceptance of another person, offer criticism very sparingly, constructively, and compassionately, and act in a manner that conveys approval. Again, if you want to increase love feelings, observe your behaviors for their consistency with that desire.

Of course, it is not likely that you can make yourself feel strongly positive toward someone you abhor simply by acting as if you love him. But acting on it can intensify a weakened love. Carl calls his wife at work and tells her, "I was just thinking of you and I wanted to say hello. Have you got time to talk?" That is an act of collaboration, the kind of small behavior that builds goodwill.

Consider it this way: Each time a relationship-promoting behavior is demonstrated, it is as if a deposit is made in a relationship account. Building up the account creates hopefulness, a positive expectation of the future. And, in fact, deposits do eventually yield interest. A high frequency of pleasing behavior creates the attitude "He [she] thinks well of me and tries to please me; I will do the same."

What's more, an account with high-deposit activity can withstand occasional withdrawals in the form of displeasing behaviors. Deposits in the form of pleasing behaviors act as buffers against the sting of displeasing behaviors. Withdrawals are inevitable, but it is only in a depleted or overdrawn account, where pleasing behaviors are too few and hopefulness has been replaced by despair, that bankruptcy is likely to occur.

The Mutual Support program provides an opportunity for you to build up your relationship account and thereby create a collaborative atmosphere, which in turn will yield positive responses.

Although the Mutual Support program may seem cumbersome, it actually proceeds quite smoothly and easily after a day or two. The rewards, for those who persevere, are worth this initial effort. Commitment to the relationship is likely to increase; new, positive exchanges are likely to form on a

Strategy Three: Develop a Culture of Collaboration 67

gradual basis without the fear that usually accompanies more drastic change efforts; blaming and "I'll change after you" patterns will be weakened; positive expectations and a renewed optimism will be generated.

Discussion Forum

Pretend that a colleague whose marriage is troubled has read this chapter. He (or she) is reluctant to institute the Mutual Support program. "Ah, it won't work"; "I don't have the time"; "My partner is not receptive" are just some of the resistance issues your colleague raises. Role-play the resistant colleague, have your partner make the best case for instituting the MSP, and then switch roles. This time you make the case while your partner plays resistant.

Now, talk about your own resistance, bring in the benefits, and continue the discussion until you have come up with a plan—either the MSP or your own version of a collaborative strategy—and commit to implementing the program.

• We have different perspectives and that is the value of our team.

PART II:

Marketing Plan and Sales Strategy

STRATEGY FOUR

Create Lasting Value

Quiet Virtues

The headlines scream: "Corporate leaders are accused of using deceptive strategies, even outright lies, when it serves their interests to get ahead!"

Recent examples include pharmaceutical companies rushing to market with a dangerous drug, influenced by its enormous profit potential; car and tire manufacturers withholding information about faulty products; major corporations hiding their losses with accounting firms that collude in the scheme; charities that give more to themselves than to the needy; companies clandestinely dumping pollutants into our environment to avoid costly waste-management expenditures; and financial institutions misleading investors.

All of this undermines value.

By contrast, a study of outstanding accountants at one of the largest firms in the United States discovered that one distinction was their willingness to stand up to their clients. They had the courage to resist the pressures at their own firms not to lose an account because they insisted on correct accounting rules. The best accountants had the integrity to stand by their values; they were the ones who inspired trust.

Trustworthiness—behaving consistently, honestly, and reliably—sets apart outstanding performers in jobs of every kind. Most firms depend on repeat business and ongoing relationships to thrive. Hiding crucial information, breaking promises, and failing to fulfill commitments are costly mistakes in business, and especially in marriage.

Here is the account of one woman who consulted with me.

It's been four years since Bob and I have not been close and I still cannot be very exact about when an awareness of trouble began in the marriage. It was very subtle, like there had been a barely perceptible eroding of the foundation, weakening my commitment in innocent increments. I began feeling like I wanted to be away from Bob more than I felt like being with him. At first I figured it was just overwork and I cut back. But that didn't really help. I couldn't pin my dissatisfaction on something. I complained about a bunch of things but in my heart I knew that wasn't it.

I knew that if I were in love with somebody, the things I complained about wouldn't be a problem. I knew that, but I was frightened to admit it to myself. The implications weren't good. For about two years I just stumbled along. There were no major confrontations between us but I wasn't happy. I started more seriously thinking about leaving. All this time Bob didn't really know the degree of my unhappiness; he thought I was just sounding off in an ordinary way. He's a good guy. I can't say he abused me or that he even did anything really bad. How do you tell him you've just fallen out of love?

Finally, out of desperation, I consulted with you. I didn't even tell Bob initially. I consulted with you for over a month before I told him. As psychologists do, you were gently insistent that we explore why I was so uncomfortable telling Bob I had begun treatment. You told me that you felt that the same dynamic was probably behind me not telling him as had brought on the trouble in the first place. And you were right. I didn't tell Bob because I just didn't feel his reaction would be sincere. He would express concern initially, but by the next week it would be as if I hadn't told him. It would be out of his mind. That's how things were with him. I regarded it as a false sincerity. No follow-up.

It's like when I told him a few months ago that I had a really important meeting at work and I was really stressed over it. He expressed real concern. Then the day of the meeting came, he said nothing. The next day, he said nothing. It was as if the issue never existed. Can he really care about me and not ask? That little example and variations on it happened numerous times. I thought I had become used to it. But after a few months of therapy I realized that it was that sort of thing that had dampened my feelings for Bob. I had been looking for some big dramatic event. It was the small things that just chipped away at my feelings.

Not only are these everyday issues difficult to identify, after a while they are often a confusing source of discomfort for the disillusioned partner. As with the woman above, it surfaces gradually and indirectly through irritation, withdrawal, or sometimes through a dramatic betrayal such as an affair. In the beginning, though, uncoupling occurs in a subtle, private manner. It is an unexpressed feeling growing in the psyche of a disgruntled lover like a deadly cancer—and it is about trust, being able to count on the other person's sincerity.

The disillusioned partner may be discomforted but he or she may fall into the same pattern as the resented partner. Affection may be expressed insincerely; clandestine support may be sought with a trusted ally. The breach is usually deepened as discontent begins to be expressed indirectly, through the words and deeds of everyday life: "I wish you would start being on time"; "I can't stand it when you speak with food in your mouth"; "How can you sit around all day and not be productive?"

The emphasis is on the other person's daily failings. The complaints are real but miss the degree of discontent. Usually, the response to the complaints match the level at which they were issued, minor grumbles are matched with grumbling retorts. And so the deception, a deception of true feelings, continues to confuse and muddle the underlying schism between the couple.

In relationships as in business, trust is like a bridge that enables us to connect with each other. Whether in business or in love relationships, we feel safe enough to attain intimacy when the bridge is solid and we are confident of its support.

When trust is undermined and we feel disappointed or betrayed, such as when we are deceived by a lie, exploited by a broken promise, or disappointed by the discrepancy between what is said and done, we pull back, just as we would do on a bridge that has become unsteady. Our expectations are shattered. We may be so shaken that trust in our own judgment is undermined. We feel a sense of loss that a loved one didn't respect us enough to be honest or fulfill a promise.

In short, the relationship becomes a weakened bridge that we can no longer cross, leaving us scrambling to get back to the safety of solid ground. In some cases, we may feel terrified that we are losing control over our lives, since we don't know where to turn for support.

Trust means different things to different people—dependability, loyalty, honesty, fidelity, predictability. But at its heart is the need to feel physically secure and emotionally safe. When you trust someone you are able to express your deepest feelings and fears; you can reveal who you are and what you need, knowing the other person will accept you, respect your feelings, and protect you. In turn, your trusting partner can do the same, knowing you will respond in kind.

Trust has a major impact among executives in the workplace. Researchers at the Center for Creative Leadership, in a study done in the 1980s and updated in the late nineties, depicted executive failures as overly ambitious, too ready to get ahead at the expense of other people. The successful executives in the study had high integrity, with a strong concern for the needs of their subordinates and colleagues. They did not impress their boss at the expense of co-workers, and they were trustworthy.

In essence, whether at home or at the office, when you trust someone and act on that trust, you are giving that person a piece of yourself, believing they will be understanding, caring, and honor your faith in them.

Some people mistakenly think of trust as something that comes into play only in crises, such as when one partner is accused of sexual infidelity. However, trust must actually be woven into the entire fabric of the relationship. We need to be able to trust in an all-inclusive way, counting on our partner to be reliable, honest, keep promises, act in our best interest, maintain confidences, and return our love. While a small, isolated breach of trust may have minor impact, repeated instances will have a cumulative effect.

Fault Lines

Sexual infidelity gets the big press and usually has devastating implications, but everyday breaches—a small lie about a purchase, a slight exaggeration about a job promotion, a cover-up about a forgotten birthday—take a bite out of emotional security. Even more devastating are deceptive patterns that undermine trust.

Annette explains:

> During the past few months I suspected something was wrong with Mike. He kept telling me everything was fine. Last week, out of the blue, he told me there was an investigation at his firm that had been going on for nearly a year and he was named in an indictment. He wanted me to know in case it made the news. I was shocked, but even more shocked that he had not confided in me earlier, that each day he came home and faked it. I feel like the past year was fraudulent. He

says he didn't want to worry me. Now I wonder if I can trust him to be honest about anything.

Annette's reaction is common. When trust is breached in one area, the disappointed partner is often so shaken that it creates an overall feeling of insecurity in the relationship. That is the power of trust betrayed. It spreads throughout the entire relationship like a deadly toxin.

In the workplace, executives who shine know that credibility stems from integrity. They are frank, acknowledging their feelings, even feelings that express shortcomings—"I have been preoccupied with my daughter's illness"—which contributes to their aura of authenticity. Being reliable and consistent, acknowledging shortcomings, promotes credibility.

In contrast, executives who are not forthright and who are unreliable undermine credibility and are destined for failure. Certainly, the same applies at home.

For instance, Kevin and Janice, two technology consultants who are both in their second marriage, are on the verge of splitting because Janice contends that Kevin "never lives up to his word." Here's what Janice told me about some troubling events:

> I can't believe anything he tells me anymore. I ask him if he's taken care of the dentist bill and he assures me that he has. The next thing I know, the dental office is calling and asking me about the overdue balance. That type of thing has happened several times already. Or I ask him to do me a favor. He agrees and then doesn't come through.

As Janice described it to me, when she complained to Kevin about his behavior, their conversation went like this:

Kevin: There you go, exaggerating again. I was only late with a bill once. Maybe twice. And I knew you'd bug me if I told you the truth. The same thing with the favors. Sometimes I say yes just so you'll get off my case.

Janice: So now you're telling me that you purposely lie to me and it's my fault because I bug you.

Kevin: I'm just saying that sometimes you drive me crazy, and at those times, especially if I'm feeling tired or something, I'll do anything to get relief.

Janice: *(sarcastically)* That's great. Now I can never trust what you tell me, because it may be one of those times that you simply want to be left alone or avoid a hassle.

At this point, Janice explained that she felt so disappointed and insecure by Kevin's lack of candor that she no longer trusted him in any area of their life and was ready to leave. Kevin pleaded with her to reconsider and she did, on the condition that she and Kevin resolve their differences.

Kevin agreed to discuss their relationship and talk honestly about what bothered him as well as listen to Janice's concerns. In their discussion it became clear that Kevin had chosen the convenience of "yessing" Janice at the expense of his credibility. By talking openly for the first time and implementing a plan to strengthen trust, they established a renewed bond.

Janice and Kevin's relationship illustrates that being inconsistent or unreliable is almost certain to undermine a relationship. Inconsistency is present when a partner speaks and acts in contradictory ways. If one partner tells the other, "You are the most important person in my life and my top priority," but in daily behavior is selfish, inconsiderate, and irritable, how can the words be trusted? Actions speak more forcefully and belie the words. Sincerity counts!

Building toward greater honesty and increased trust involves not simply saying what one believes, but doing what one says. A person who wants to be counted on must be reliable and consistent in both words and behaviors. One must "walk the walk," as they say.

Frequently, partners who have difficulties following through on their word are motivated by temporary feelings of guilt ("She seems so upset, I'd better do this") or require the approval of their partner ("I'd better say yes; he seems terribly angry about this"). Others acquiesce so that their partner will get off their backs. As we've seen with Janice and Kevin, the relief is short-lived, only to be replaced by their partner's rage.

The same effect is often produced by vague statements: "I agree that I need to be more attentive" or "Okay, I'll be more responsive." In the former the speaker does not indicate a willingness to do something different; the latter statement avoids a specific plan of action and is likely to be just another empty statement that weakens trust.

On other occasions, suspicion arises not so much from what is said, but by how it is said. Larry may say to his wife, "I'm listening," while glancing at the morning newspaper. Rita, Larry's wife, has good cause to wonder about the reliability of Larry's statement, as he was obviously more interested in the morning's news than in conversing with Rita. Larry could have said, "Couldn't we wait till later?" If Rita felt strongly about talking, she could have made this known. If she didn't, she could have respected Larry's desire to delay the conversation.

Larry and Rita were being overly polite in an attempt to create an impression that is unreasonable: We are both *always* desirous of contact with each other. In actuality, both Larry and Rita were collecting resentment and undermining the trust in the relationship.

The Great Divide

There's nothing like a secret for undermining trust. Secrets come in all sizes, degrees of complexity, and forms, and they are not uncommon. In a poll of one thousand married people published in *Reader's Digest* (August, 2001), more than three-quarters had kept secrets from their spouses.

Here is an illustration of a woman whose secret began over what would seem to be a minor issue, but for her it was consuming. Dolores is in her late thirties and she grew up in a household that was very guarded. The talk around her dinner table was about things, not people and not feelings. If ever there was discussion of personal issues, it was about the foolishness of a neighbor or friend who revealed too much of themselves.

Dolores was married to a man heavily involved with his electronics company and his executive staff. She secretly resented the attention he lavished on his colleagues to the exclusion of her. She was ashamed that she felt the way she did because she was raised to believe that work came first and that her role was to bring happiness to her husband. Her anguish was exacerbated when her husband would spend what little time he gave her each evening talking of the day he had at work.

Each night she considered discussing her feelings with her husband and each night she talked herself out of it. "He is a good man," she told herself. "He works hard, and he has done so much for me. How could I interfere with his business? I am just being selfish!"

One evening while her husband was working late, Dolores went to the local mall to do some shopping. She was in one of the large stores when her heart began to palpitate, her breathing became rapid and shallow, and she felt as if she were going to faint. Dolores dropped the merchandise she had been considering, ran to her car, and rushed home. She was having what was later described as an anxiety attack.

At first she thought she was just tired, or perhaps she hadn't eaten enough, but when the attacks became more frequent she consulted with her family physician who referred her to a psychiatrist. The psychiatrist prescribed medication, but Dolores wasn't satisfied taking medication. For a time she coped by staying close to home and making sure that she ate properly and slept sufficiently. Despite her efforts, her ability to function became increasingly limited and required that her husband be with her more and pay closer attention to her.

Initially, her husband responded to her requests with consideration, but as time passed and her condition worsened, his patience began to wear thin. One night, after her husband witnessed Dolores in the middle of an anxiety attack, he became so upset that he insisted she consult with a psychologist. When she refused, he threatened to leave her if she didn't do something to get better. He insisted he could not keep up with a reduced work schedule and "hold her hand" indefinitely.

After her initial consult with me I requested that she bring her husband to the next meeting. "Why?" she asked defensively. "It is my problem. What does my husband have to do with it?"

"When you are able to talk to your husband about the feelings you are hiding from him, your anxiety will start improving," I suggested, having quickly realized that her symptom was speaking for her. In effect, her attacks were saying to her husband: "I need more of you, but I can't express it. Will you listen to my pain?"

It wasn't until several visits later that Dolores finally found the courage to express all the secret resentments she harbored about her husband's over-involvement with his business and his under-involvement with her. Her husband was shocked but open to hearing her complaints. It took several months of further discussion before balance was restored to their marriage. Just as I had suggested, Dolores's anxiety gradually diminished until, nearly a year later, her smile returned and her anxiety was completely resolved.

Dolores's secret was something others might not be ashamed of, but secrets are something few of us are unfamiliar with. All of us have experienced secretiveness in different forms. In some cases withholding can go to the heart of the relationship. These include instances in which one person keeps secret certain very personal pieces of information, or the existence of a hidden life, even criminal behavior.

Common forms of withholding involve gambling, drinking or other substance abuse problems. Often, people don't speak honestly of the extent of their difficulties with these behaviors. Problems in this area usually involve minimizing, denial, lying, and cover-ups, all usually requiring professional intervention.

Disclosure generally shocks the uninformed partner. That's what happened to Katherine after she had been married to Jack, a prosperous businessman, for eight years. One day, upon returning from work, Jack suddenly announced, "I'm declaring bankruptcy. My business is going under because I have had to mortgage it to the hilt to pay off gambling losses." He explained that he had been trying to negotiate his way out of his losses for a year and he wanted to tell her before she read about his company going under.

Jack's revelation hit Katherine like a bolt of lightning, and she felt betrayed that he hadn't told her sooner. She had been aware that he had been preoccupied and inattentive for the last few months, and she had believed him when he explained that he just had some difficult problems at work. His seemingly reasonable explanation led her to think he was dealing with something ordinary and routine, certainly not a major financial disaster.

What else had he held back? What other secrets did he have that would shock her? Here's what Jack told me about his behavior.

> I really screwed up. Katherine is right to feel that I closed her out of my troubles. For me, it has been a way of life. I am not proud to admit it, but this is the way I've operated for years and years—for as long as I can remember. In my family my mother led us kids to believe that our father couldn't take any bad news. Growing up, we learned to keep our problems from him. Either we wouldn't tell Dad at all, or we'd water things down so he wouldn't be upset. When I wanted to go to my mother with something, my sister would nix it. She told me that my mother had enough to worry about since my father didn't deal with half of what was going on. So, I didn't talk to my mother or father and my sister was older than me, she was into guys and was never around. I got used to holding secrets and continued that in my relationship with Katherine.

Not surprisingly, as an adult, Jack tended not to worry his wife with anything that might cause her concern. In therapy, and Gambler's Anonymous meetings, which Jack attended at Katherine's insistence, Jack came to realize that his secrecy not only deprived Katherine from really knowing him but also deprived him of Katherine's support. What's more, since he kept anything really important about himself secret, there was never much to talk to her about. As Katherine said, "He was slowly turning into a stranger."

After two months in therapy, Jack announced to Katherine that he was going to the doctor because he was feeling some discomfort in his stomach. Since his uncle and his father had had stomach cancer he wanted to check it out. Fortunately, Jack got a clean bill of health. The experience was a real turning point for him. In the past he would not have told her about his concern. "I was really worried and Katherine was wonderfully supportive," he said. "I feel like I am part of a loving family and it is a really good feeling. I feel pounds lighter, so much more relaxed. And we have so much more to talk about now!"

Frisky Business

As distraught as Katherine was over Jack's deceptiveness about his gambling and finances, the reaction when one partner discovers that the other is having an affair is often unequaled by the revelation of other secrets: profound shock followed by hurt, anger, and a complete shattering of trust. Affairs are the great trustbusters.

Despite the danger of sexual harassment, there's a lot of loving going on in the office. Given endless work weeks and the integration of the workforce (now 46 percent female), the office provides the perfect environment for attractions to form. Coworkers have similar traits and goals, are familiar and accessible, and share in each other's excitement, frustrations, and celebrations.

In other words, work is a turn-on. You shower, dress up in a power suit, and go to a place where you are valued for your ideas, energy, and ability to get things done. You hang around other people who are also at their best and brightest. Then you're thrown into situations that get the adrenaline flowing; spending long hours together under intense circumstances.

If opportunities are limited at work, or better judgment prevails, at least with regard to meeting a paramour at the office, there is always the Internet. Along with several million porn sites, the Internet has accommodated illicit desire with several sites for coupled men and women. Sites like "Married and Flirting" at Yahoo, a chat room dedicated to those who are married but itchy, are gaining in popularity.

Online romances have a special appeal for married women who are too busy to leave the house. They can flirt, tease, and not take the time to dress up, all the while getting the attention that they do not receive from their partners. But as popular as online flirting is, it is the office romance that is burgeoning.

Exhibit A is the well-publicized early 1980s relationship between Bendix Corporation president William Agee and his then executive assistant, Mary Cunningham. Agee had promoted Cunningham from executive assistant to vice president, to the outrage of other Bendix employees. Then Agee's relationship with Mary Cunningham burst into the news.

Their affair, replete with power, brains, youth, good looks, charm, denial, and deceit, fascinated the American public. Cunningham was forced to leave Bendix to work for Seagrams, with the entire country wondering just how well she would do. The two divorced their respective spouses and married soon thereafter.

The romance had a happy ending: The Agees were married in 1982, and for their reception they commissioned an ice sculpture of two adjoining hands, symbolizing "the bonds of business partnership and matrimony."

More often, however, relationships are broken, not renewed, by affairs. Consider the experience of a very attractive, intense, twice-married woman I spoke with who is approaching forty. She works long hours but makes sure she is available in the evening for time with her husband. He doesn't seem interested.

> Being a product of my times, I used sex with another man as a weapon. My husband works long hours when he really doesn't have to, and I resent it. In the past, I always made it a point to get home at a reasonable hour. When he comes home, he is preoccupied. He wants to watch television, read, sleep, or go on his boat. That boat is driving me crazy. I don't want to compete with a goddamn boat! I feel he would choose that boat over me without a moment of hesitation. I don't feel married. It seems he regards me as a convenience. When he is attentive, it is often in a belittling and critical manner; he makes me feel stupid and ridiculous.
>
> One time I was relining the shelves in one of the closets very meticulously because I like things to be perfect and beautiful, and he nagged me something awful and called me a fool for wasting my time on something no one would ever see. So either he pesters me or he ignores me. I've tried talking to him about it but he dismisses me. To deal with my feelings I have lovers. And then, when my husband continues

to ignore me, to take me for granted, or comes on with his criticisms, I sit back, smile inside, and say to myself, "You're not so hot, you fool." That's my revenge!

There is a pattern to the men I pursue at work. First, I'll find myself noticing something about his physical appearance. Then, I'll ruminate over some personal data about him. The person may appear in my dreams. I begin to ask him questions about himself, watch how he is with other people, perhaps get in conversations with friends at work about who's cute or not, and think of him, perhaps giggling at his joke more. I'll initiate more conversations with him. I may covertly pass on information about my availability. I move into a more personal state and seek contact with him outside the workplace.

That was working well for me, as bad as it sounds. Then my husband found out. A friend of his told him, and although he didn't believe it at first, he became suspicious. He hired a detective who followed me and took pictures of my lover and me. The pictures were very graphic. When my husband saw the pictures he threw up on the spot. He came home and exploded; he was enraged. He pulled one of the wooden posts right off the bed and began smashing things. The room looked as if a bomb exploded in it. I ran to call the police and he ripped the phone off the wall. He went nuts. The next day he locked himself in the garage and ran the car; he attempted suicide. It was then that I really felt badly. That's when I realized how much I had hurt him and how much pain he was in.

The woman describing her experience told me she was discovered because she told a friend of hers about her affair, her friend told her husband, and he then told the affair-involved woman's husband. Affairs are big secrets that, once revealed, have very strong consequences. That's part of the problem; affairs don't lend themselves to sharing and openness. In ever-widening circles, it causes the person involved to operate in a cautious manner in their primary relationship, and with others as well. Being guarded deteriorates trust. In contrast, openness supports trust.

In addition to the trust-eroding reticence, deception, and lying that are part of an affair, there is usually a change in attitude and behavior at home that arouses a mate's suspicions. Some of the affair-involved distance themselves from their mate, playing out a loyalty to their lovers. Others become more amorous in an effort to compensate for their dalliance. Still others behave uncharacteristically in a variety of ways and inadvertently deflate whatever emotional safety remains in the relationship.

Diane, an executive recruiter for a large placement firm, is in her early forties. She has been married eighteen years and described a period in her life to me when she had two affairs, both office romances.

> Although these experiences were meaningful to me, they were far from dramatic. I did not experience a grand awakening and I wasn't particularly enamored of my sexual partners. Yet I was excited and there was a change in me that I thought I was concealing successfully. I wasn't. One Sunday morning my husband turned to me in bed and said, "I know people change as they grow, but when you live with a woman for such a long time, you get to know her very well; you relate to me in a certain way. In the past few months, a change has come over you. I don't know what to make of it. I don't know what's wrong, but you don't seem to be with me in the same way. Did I do something to provoke this?

While this kind of response may occur more often than would ordinarily be predicted, some affairs may go undiscovered for a lifetime. Nonetheless, the adulterous party takes a greater risk if the outside relationship is very involved, since there will more likely be subtle—and not so subtle—changes in behavior and attitude.

Typically, at this juncture the adulterous mate will begin to escalate the lying: "Oh, it's my business troubles," or "I'm just edgy, I need a rest." If his or her mate does not buy these ambiguous answers, and suspicion continues to be aroused, the lying increases as the secret expands—and the trust continues to deteriorate.

And yes, sometimes a lover seeking to make trouble at home and force a separation leaves the evidence. The affair-involved person may also sabotage him- or herself. A diary kept, letters not destroyed, sometimes an indiscreet choice of meeting places—do these have a deliberate element?

Sexual betrayal itself is bad enough—a nuclear assault on the non-involved partner—but sometimes this most serious breach may contain an unconscious message. In some relationships the affair may be a way of forcing the hand of a mate who refuses to acknowledge that the relationship is in trouble. Detection may also serve the purpose of those who want their mate to dissolve the relationship.

Thus, in an empty relationship, a mate may flaunt infidelity to provoke a breakup—it becomes an open secret. When the relationship is merely troubled, an affair that is left open to discovery may be a signal to the indifferent partner to pay more attention to the relationship. Of course, most people do not willingly acknowledge that the brazenness of their sexual betrayal conveys such purposes.

Nor is the intended effect usually achieved. A man who is indiscreetly conducting an affair may wish to punish his partner for past grievances; but the partner may respond with more hostility than he bargained for, perhaps with an affair of her own. A woman who is trying to push her partner into being more attentive may find herself alone when he walks out on her. In some cases the hurt partner may be completely devastated and react very strongly, perhaps violently, or attempt to harm him- or herself.

Occasionally, an individual will deny a mate's obvious affair involvement because acknowledgment may be so threatening to his or her sense of emotional security that it cannot be tolerated. Thus, the non-involved and the involved partner enter into a conspiracy of silence about the big secret.

Don Blank, a large man with imposing stature, is a business consultant specializing in the auto industry. He is in his early forties and he is very involved in his work; his idea of relaxing on the weekend is to read an auto industry report and take notes. He barely notices that his wife is out many evenings and often comes home in disarray with alcohol on her breath; he doesn't react to hang-ups when he picks up the phone, nor does he complain that she is rarely interested in being sexual with him, despite her interest in watching sex scenes in movies and reading sexy stories. He seems to have unconsciously entered into a trade-off: his lover is his work, hers is an actual person, and he doesn't want to know any more than that.

A fair number of men and women employ the same defense of denial. Rather than confront the truth, they unconsciously join in keeping the secret and establishing a pseudo-relationship wherein the satisfaction derived from outside activities masks the emptiness within. Frequent entertaining and extravagant dining out, relocating, elaborate decorating, and job-hopping can be attempts made by the couple to fill the void.

In contrast to a marriage that is weighed down by unresolved trust issues, I have met both men and women who have voluntarily and self-servingly confessed their extramarital dalliances. Their purpose is not to clear the air and begin a healing process; it is to create distance and alienate their partner. For some people, the fear of being engulfed is even stronger than their fear of abandonment.

In still other instances, a partner may confess an illicit sexual relationship to save the marriage. The confession serves to defuse the attraction of the other person and to create more vigilance in their partner so that a future fall from grace is less likely. It doesn't always work out that way. Maureen, an account exec at a major ad firm, had this to say.

> I was so hurt and angered by my husband's affair that I did nothing for four days but cry. My face was puffy and raw. I couldn't hold food; my weight fell well below normal. After those initial days—I refer to them now as the days of mourning—I started to plot and scheme. I tried to think of the best way of getting back. Howard has a brother. He is two years younger; he and his brother have been competitive all their lives. I know his brother finds me attractive. He's even made passes at me. I decided to seduce him. It worked without a hitch; his brother was most cooperative. Of course, when I told Howard he felt as if someone had driven a truck through his stomach. I thought that would teach him. However, about six months later he got involved with one of my friends. That was it, we divorced.

Healing is more likely to be furthered through a series of painful discussions than through denial. However, the cost of confessing a sexual betrayal is obvious, immediate, and long-term. Once told, a couple will have to live with the repercussions for a long time to come.

In telling, we deal not only with our partner's rage and pain, but also with a lengthy process of rebuilding intimacy—if it is to be rebuilt at all. So, to tell or not to tell, that is an important question. When suspicion arising out of unfaithfulness is a barrier to intimacy and the deceived partner continues to probe the issue, a frank discussion, preferably with the assistance of a therapist, is warranted.

Of course, even at this juncture some people may choose not to be candid. A person remaining with a partner for expediency's sake—for instance, a wife with several children who has no hope of employment, and who wants nothing from the marriage except financial support—may continue to lie in an effort to maintain the relationship. But those who wish to improve things would best consider honesty. When suspicion has become part of the marital relationship, further deception will only serve to create more distance, mistrust, and disillusion.

Some people do not reveal their secret because they want to continue the affair. They want to have both their lover and their spouse, and they know that a confession will force a choice. Others have trouble dealing with emotional turmoil and want to avoid the substantial repair process that is required following disclosure. Still others may lack the strength and sense of commitment to face their partner's accusations and the loss of face they will experience.

Confessions, like all things, may be for better or worse. Ordinarily, the chances are better for confessions that have more noble motives and worse for those that are self-serving. The self-serving reasons include using the truth about an affair as an exit visa from an unhappy marriage; revealing the affair as a weapon of revenge; using the affair to shake up a lethargic marriage. All of these reasons for confessing have too much of a self-centered basis. There are better, less hurtful ways of approaching a marriage in trouble. If the unhappiness, for example, is overwhelming and beyond repair, just leave! If there is a lot of anger in the relationship, why not address that, and the underlying hurt (it's always there!) rather than focusing on hurting your mate?

In telling, the best motive is the wish to re-establish the primacy of your marriage and to remove the barrier of the kept secret. And make no mistake about it, the effects of silence about a secret life take a toll on intimacy. The telling begins an emotional journey that is arduous and not for the faint of heart. However, by repairing trust we also open the door for an atmosphere of emotional safety and for more depth and closeness in a relationship.

To tell or not to tell? Couple therapists disagree. Some suggest that telling is a nonnegotiable first step toward restoring closeness. They maintain that secrecy is a form of crazy-making. Telling the truth serves the critical function of precipitating a needed marital crisis and creates the opportunity for honest dialogue. Other therapists contend that the risks are too great and advise against it unless the suspicion is so high as to warrant the risks.

My view is not hard and fast. In some situations, for some couples, the secret is best revealed. It can be the start of a new and better relationship. In other instances, the consequences can be so destructive that repair is next to impossible. In some ways it is like being told about a cancer diagnosis. Some people recover better when they are told every detail of their condition and their treatment, others are overcome by what they know and exceedingly frightened and distraught.

Again, those that confess with the motive of moving the relationship to a higher plane are more likely to achieve that goal. Whether silence is chosen or a confession is made, no matter how the secret is handled, there are consequences.

To maximize trust it is wise to follow a simple rule in a love relationship: Don't do anything you can't share, and be prepared to discuss everything you do. Secrets, especially ones that may involve daily deception, are sure to create distance. It is not possible to foster trust with someone you are hiding from, confusing, and throwing off track.

Tool Kit

There are two main ways for the offender (and the offended) to make things worse when confronted with a trust violation. One is withdrawal, to keep everything bottled up inside. The other is to erupt, to emote without restraint. If you are having too many conversations with yourself, you are probably not having enough with your partner. If you are screaming, hurling insults, and looking to vent without concern for the impact, not briefly, but more often, the relationship is certain to deteriorate.

Bear in mind: A critical action on the trust-breaker's part, as reassurance that his efforts to restore trust are sincere, is his willingness to delve into himself, confront the personal issues that lead to trust breaches, and acknowledge them openly and responsibly.

To begin, an unequivocal apology is in order. No excuses, no buts, no mitigating circumstances. The apology should be something like, "I am very sorry that I behaved in an irresponsible manner, that I betrayed your faith in me by deceiving you." It is not something like, "I'm sorry you're upset about my gambling but if you didn't make me so nervous about money I wouldn't have taken such risks to pay the bills."

The former is the statement of an adult who realizes that he is in charge of his life, and the consequences of his actions. The latter is the statement of a child who still believes that he is a victim of other people or circumstances. Unless he changes his view and begins to take charge of his life, the chances that he will be a trustworthy partner are near zero. Other considerations:

1. Following an apology is the discussion or more likely a series of discussions with the goal of understanding the basis for trust violations. Simply stated, "Why has this happened, and what is going to happen that will

prevent a recurrence?" Understanding the basis for a breach of trust does not guarantee that it won't happen again. However, unless there is a belief in magic, it is unreasonable to assume that trust violations will not recur without addressing the reasons they have occurred and formulating a prevention plan.
2. Some questions to pose for a discussion: What influences from our family of origin may be undermining our relationship? What changes need to be made in the relationship to strengthen the trust and intimacy? Very specifically, what kinds of behaviors are acceptable and what are out of bounds? Can the damage be repaired? What, specifically, will it take? What are the hopes and expectations for the future?
3. While talking is critical, it is not enough. Behavioral patterns require change as well. In the past, for example, the partner who has violated the trust may have come home at night, barely mumbled a hello as he was reviewing the mail, made some small talk during dinner, and retired to the TV to watch the ballgame for the remainder of the evening. That routine, not much of a relationship promoter under any circumstance, definitely won't cut it in the wake of a breach of trust.
4. The offending partner needs to think through exactly what he'd like to see happen in the relationship and behave in a manner that promotes his vision. Regardless of the specifics, the general message his behavior should convey is, "I love you. You matter to me. I want to demonstrate that I am trustworthy." This may require a shift in the usual manner of behaving and in the daily routine. It can be a lot of work, a real stretch for some people. If a serious trust issue is to be repaired it can only happen in the context of a caring environment. It is up to the offending partner to create that atmosphere, even if it is at some sacrifice.
5. The reparative behaviors required might be new and challenging, but they do not have to be sensational. Indeed, some people are so preoccupied with major shifts that opportunities for small but important gestures are overlooked. Others mistakenly believe that a repair process moves along on its own energy and consequently do not bother to fuel it at all. These individuals are similar to those who seem to sidestep escalating conflict by sweeping the incident under the rug and acting as if it hadn't occurred. It may appear as if conflict has been safely avoided in these instances. Appearances notwithstanding, there is no avoidance of trust violations without negative consequences.
6. Just as relationship-supporting behaviors need to be strengthened, there

are also trust-specific requirements to be considered. Common requests are for greater accountability, consistency, reliability, and sacrifice. Especially in instances where there has been an affair or uncontrolled gambling or substance abuse, accountability may involve an accurate itinerary during travel, calls during the day, and coming home from work in time to have dinner with the family. It goes without saying that the trust-violating behavior in question must stop completely. No more contact with a lover, for example. Doing whatever it takes to give up drugs or alcohol, including detox, recovery meetings or in-patient treatment, if needed, is essential.

7. In addition to accountability, most trust-damaged lovers require consistency and reliability to be present in a much greater degree than had been the case previously. Being clear about intentions and keeping agreements, even those that seem minor, such as calling when promised, are very important. Once the trust wound has been exposed, sensitivity is increased and must be respected.

8. Some couples also request that monthly bank statements, credit card statements, and phone bills are made available. Other couples insist on therapy, and a complete and detailed description of the trust violations. Yet others need some time for intimate talk and reassurance each day. The specific requests vary from person to person, but in all cases they should be honored in the interest of helping the hurt partner feel more cared for, appreciated, and emotionally secure. And that's how the trust-breaking partner should view them, rather than as punitive, and arbitrary.

9. Strengthening trust is not a one-person endeavor. The offended partner shares in the responsibility of the repair process. In fact, if there isn't receptiveness to the possibility of trusting again, and an encouragement of the offender's efforts to restore confidence, the process is destined to fail. An indefinite sentence or a prolonged period of coldness and alienation, perhaps going on for months, will almost surely result in the offended partner giving up in his efforts to reconnect. It is most helpful, in contrast, to consider carefully what is needed to restore trust, spell it out (not globally, like "be more reliable," but specifically, like, "call when you say you will") and collaborate with the offender in creating a blueprint for reparation.

Realistically, being responsive to an offending partner's efforts when there has been a betrayal or pattern of deception is a major challenge. In these instances, the negative cycle is well established and will not yield easily: simply thinking about the relationship differently, although important, is not powerful enough. More is needed. Behavior must change and *both* partners must be committed to the repair process. It takes two to put the repair of trust on a healing path.

Discussion forum

Take turns bringing up one of your smaller trust issues and discuss it fully. The offender is to take clear responsibility for his or her part. Not only will the offender discuss what happened in detail, he or she will dig deeply into the basic causes of the trust-damaging behavior. The partner on the receiving end, the one whose trust has been violated, will listen carefully with a forgiving attitude—that person's turn to be the "confessor" is next.

What is the role of the offended? Besides listening with compassion, consider that in relationships a system is formed and both partners play a part. One partner may be the offender, but the other is also influential in the system. For example, there can be no dominating husband without a submissive wife, no interrupting wife without a passive husband.

Emotional safety will make our relationship more passionate.

STRATEGY FIVE

Become a Skillful Communicator

Mood and Meaning

In striking contrast to the enthusiasm of courtship, conversation in many post-honeymoon relationships becomes painfully strained:

She: You never talk to me.
He: What's on your mind?
She: It's that I never know what's on *your* mind.
He: What do you want to know?
She: Everything!
He: That's ridiculous.
She: *(angrily)* Is talking to that blond assistant of yours ridiculous?
He: Come on, cut it out.
She: *(on the verge of tears)* You never talk to me the way you did when we first met.
He: Here we go again.

The biggest single complaint of American workers is poor communication with management. According to a report published in *Newsweek* (August 12, 1996), two-thirds of workers polled say it prevents them from doing their best work.

The same applies at home—in spades! There is impressive research showing rather conclusively that skillful communication is an essential element of an intimate relationship.

In its most comprehensive definition, "to communicate" means to make known; to give to another; to exchange thoughts, feelings, and information; to share; to develop a connecting link. Connecting on an intimate basis requires that both people in a relationship reveal themselves in a personal manner. In many relationships, though, an opposite process, one of restricted communication, occurs: "What he doesn't know won't hurt him." "Why bother my wife with professional or business issues she really doesn't understand?" "Better not say anything, he has enough to worry about."

In the workplace, managers who have a closed door policy, who do not appear approachable, are severely disadvantaged because they are not attuned to their subordinates' feelings. Although that attitude is negatively consequential at work, in love relationships the stakes are even higher. Feelings are the voice of the heart. Certainly the intellect plays a significant role in love, but it is the heart that speaks most powerfully. When feelings speak, we are compelled to listen, and sometimes act, even if we do not always understand why.

Knowing your feelings and being able to express them sensitively is an enormous advantage in any kind of relationship. The corollary is that not being aware of your feelings, or not knowing how to use or express them, is a handicap, particularly in a love relationship.

Unfortunately, there are many forces that combine to make awareness and expression of feelings something other than a simple matter. Sure, when you are drowning in feeling, what you are experiencing is hard to ignore; the grand passions, for better or worse, are grabbers. But life is made up of experiences that aren't dramatic. Everyday feelings are mushy, difficult to discern, non-palpable, slippery things. They are easy to misread or overlook. Beginning in childhood, many of us learn to hide or mistrust our feelings.

Here are some sample exchanges. They come from a Mommy and Me group I visited a number of years ago.

> **Child:** Mommy, I'm hungry.
> **Mommy:** You can't be. You just ate.
> **Child:** *(louder)* But I'm hungry.
> **Mommy:** You're not hungry. You're just a little grumpy.
> **Child:** *(wailing)* No, I'm hungry!
>
> **Child:** Mommy, it's hot in here.
> **Mommy:** It's chilly. Keep your sweater on.

Child: But I'm hot.
Mommy: It is not hot. Keep your sweater on!
Child: No, I'm hot.

Child: I don't like this game, it's boring.
Mommy: No, it isn't. It's very interesting.
Child: It's stupid.
Mommy: It's fun and you can learn from it.
Child: It stinks and I don't like it.
Mommy: Yes, you do.

At such moments children learn deep lessons. One obvious conclusion from these exchanges might well be that the mother doesn't care about her child's feelings. Suppose you were the child who was hungry, hot, or bored? And suppose you wanted that all-important grownup in your life to know what you were feeling?

Instead of being understanding the grownup was telling you repeatedly not to trust your own perceptions, but to rely on hers. After a time it is likely you would be hesitant to express your feelings for fear of being wrong. If you concluded that you were wrong, how could you avoid concluding that your feelings don't matter?

Very few adults can recount a childhood where their feelings, especially those that provoked their parents, were accepted. Although we are different and are capable of having different feelings without being right or wrong, it is rare that parents are able to recognize and validate our feelings.

That is the beginning; it is the point when we start to disown our feelings, especially those that we have been taught are unacceptable. And with that we lose a part of ourselves. We also divert our energy. It takes energy to block an emotion and it takes energy to free one.

As adults, we are busy. We have goals to reach, achievements to attain; and days pass quickly without much attention to feelings. Your job may be shaky, one of your children may be sick, and you may have a cold coming on, but if a casual friend asks in passing how you feel, you will probably reply, "I'm fine." This kind of superficial exchange is merely a sign of friendliness, not an expression of feelings.

Life is full of such rituals, of harmless small talk. The trouble is that over the years these shallow, habitual responses become so ingrained that they combine with our childhood experiences and make it easier to devalue the importance of feelings.

Consider this: You are at work and you have just completed a big project. You worked your heart out on the project, giving it your very best effort, and secretly suspect that the project manager is going to shower you with accolades. In fact, you are hoping that the success of your efforts will propel your career to a new level. After lunch you are called into the manager's office.

The anointing hour has arrived. The first thing you notice is the glum look on the manager's face. Although he is never upbeat, he looks more dour than usual. The meeting goes from bad to worse in a hurry. You are devastated. Your manager's final words to you are that he expects a better effort next time, and when you start to reply he puts his hand up and asserts, "I am not in the mood for excuses. This meeting is over!"

As soon as you arrive home you spill the whole story to your partner, and you get a well-intentioned but off-the-mark response. "Honey, there's no reason to be upset. Warren [the project manager] is an ass. He's always negative and you are taking him too seriously."

In this instance the person responding indirectly invalidated your feelings, not unlike the examples of mothers and children. You felt dismissed, and may back off from talking about sensitive issues.

Not dealing with feelings comes at a steep price. As the maxim goes, if you don't deal with your feelings, your feelings will deal with you. A lifetime of inattentiveness to feelings is strikingly demonstrated by Phil, an accountant, and Marla, his wife of twenty years. Two months before this conversation, Marla had asked Phil for a separation. The exchange below took place in my office.

> **Phil:** I've never felt able to be open with you about the things that really bothered me, the most personal things.
> **Marla:** I realize that. I felt the same way about being open with you. But I've pushed myself and encouraged you to do the same. I'm lonely with you. I wanted to be more passionate with you, less reserved; but I always felt you didn't really want that.
> **Phil:** *(stunned)* But, Marla, I never knew that. Why didn't you tell me how you felt? Why didn't you say something?
> **Marla:** I've told you how I felt and you didn't respond. After a few

rounds of that I just stopped. I thought that was the way you wanted things. Why didn't *you* ever say anything?

Phil: *(crying)* For the same reasons, I suppose. I took it for granted that you were happy with the status quo. I just didn't get it. God, I wish I had listened more carefully back then, Marla!

Blind Spots

The waste of time, energy, and potential happiness through the years of Marla and Phil's marriage, when what they both *really* wanted was so much more similar than what each *supposed* the other wanted, is appalling. Yet this same kind of waste characterizes millions of relationships.

Herein lies a major reason for relationship failure. While it is fashionable nowadays to complain about communication problems, many couples, influenced by the folklore of romantic love, believe that an innate sensitivity should link them and their partner. Being in a relationship, some contend, affords them the privilege of being less diligent in their efforts to communicate than they might be with their casual contacts.

In effect, they say, "You ought to know how I feel or what I mean if you really love me." Unfortunately, this is often not the case. One of the most thought-provoking results of the considerable research done in this area is knowledge of how little husbands and wives really do know or understand one another. "I know him [her] like the back of my hand," brags a husband or wife. Yet, under experimental conditions, their performance more closely resembles the comical, embarrassingly inaccurate mates of *The Newlywed Game* than teammates who correctly assess each other's signals.

Even in the simplest of predictions of each other's behavior, couples are usually wrong. In a report published in *Marriage and Family Living,* researchers asked spouses which one of them would tend to talk more during a decision-making process dealing with how they would spend a hypothetical gift of several hundred dollars. The session was recorded so that the actual amount of talking done by each could be measured.

Only seventeen out of fifty individuals correctly calculated who would be the more active negotiator. What's more, after the session was over and the participants were once again asked who talked more, over half still judged incorrectly.

In another study, investigators increased the participants' motivation to forecast correctly by presenting an assortment of items—gloves, scarves, lingerie, belts, wallets—some suitable for men, some for women. If, without communication, they could successfully coordinate their choices—that is, choose the same item—they would receive the items as rewards. They all failed. Not one of the twenty-five participating couples succeeded in predicting one another's choices on as many as five of all twenty items.

In still another study, this time involving 116 couples, each partner was asked separately to give the names of persons considered by both spouses to be close mutual friends, not including relatives. In an astonishing result, only six couples were in total accord on this task, while one couple was in complete disagreement regarding their mutual friends.

Not surprisingly, couples that have a solid, communicative relationship understand each other better than those who are unhappily married. One study of eighty-two happily married couples and eighty unsatisfactorily married couples revealed that nearly three-quarters of the former but less than half of the latter couples agreed in their answers to an elaborate 128-item questionnaire concerned with their perceptions of themselves and of their spouses.

It may be that husbands and wives have a good understanding of each other because the marital relationship is communicative to begin with, or they may enhance their communication because they have a good understanding of each other, or both.

Whatever the direction of the association, a major feature in relationships lacking in intimacy is a deficiency in communication skills. In discordant relationships, there is a marked failure of men and women to express and be attuned to each other's feelings and thoughts.

There may be any number of reasons for this plight. If raised in an uncommunicative family, an individual may have not developed adequate verbal skills. Some people are shy; they may lack self-confidence: "Why should anyone want to listen to me? I have nothing important to say." Some are intimidated, while others are hostile and do not communicate in order not to antagonize.

Still others are suspicious, self-protective, and, hence, secretive. Most often the deterioration of communication occurs gradually and is the result of an interactive process. John doesn't bring up issues for discussion because he finds Mary too critical of him. Mary is then critical of John's silence. John then concludes that he was right about Mary all along: She is a nag. Sometimes a partner will encourage communication and then discourage it by frequently interrupting, in effect, disqualifying the speaker and his or her message.

While constrained communication results in relationship dissatisfaction, this is not to say that unbridled self-expression is synonymous with marital bliss. Indeed, there is a wealth of information to suggest that uncensored communication may be more than any relationship can bear.

Such factors as timing, the interest of the other person, appropriateness, and the effects of the disclosures on either party must be considered. If a connection exists between self-expression and relationship satisfaction, research trends suggest it is curvilinear, not linear; that is, too much disclosure and too little disclosure may be associated with discord, while some intermediate amount, under appropriate conditions, is related to satisfaction.

More specifically, behavioral scientists have found that the impact of negative statements on people is greater than that of positive statements. "I really like you," in other words, is more than canceled out by "Drop dead." It may be that human beings are naturally and inherently more alert to negative cues. Being vigilant to negative and threatening cues in our environment may have proven adaptive (survival) value, and is possibly built into our psychological structure.

Whatever the explanation, the effect of too much negativity is similar to the princess who was able to focus on the pea underneath the feather bed on which she lay. The prevalence of negative expression, no matter how well intended or how eloquently expressed, draws attention away from positives and is going to have a relationship-eroding effect.

Is all this to say that honesty between a man and a woman had better be thrown to the wind? No, this is not the point. It is simply that blunt and brutal honesty seldom facilitates intimacy. Real intimacy is experienced only when people have the capacity and wisdom to be sensitive to their partner's feelings.

Tuning In

A very powerful method for countering our tendency to talk around or avoid feelings is empathic listening and response. A finely tuned ear is at the heart of empathy. Listening well is not only essential for marital success; it is also a critical element in the workplace. As reported by Anthony Carnavale and his colleagues, in *Workplace Basics: The Skills Employers Want*, the U.S. Department of Labor estimates that of the total time we spend in communication, 22 percent is devoted to reading and writing, 23 percent to speaking—and a whopping 55 percent to listening.

Listening and listening well are not to be confused, however. To understand thoroughly another person's thoughts and feelings and to be understood thoroughly by this person in return are among the most rewarding of human experiences and, unfortunately, all too rare.

Empathic listening exemplifies listening well.

Empathy is made up of two main components. One is listening and attempting to understand another's view rather than busily preparing a rebuttal; the second is communicating this understanding to the speaker. The focus in both listening and responding is on the feelings, expressed and implied. At the very least, empathy requires being able to read another person's emotions; at a higher level, it involves sensing and responding to a person's unspoken concerns or feelings. At the highest levels, empathy is understanding the issues or concerns that lie behind another person's feelings.

An experience that frequently helps to develop this pattern of communicating is role reversal. With role reversal, when a discussion involving conflict over personal/emotional issues occurs, it becomes the responsibility of each party to state the partner's position and feelings until she (or he) is satisfied with the degree of understanding achieved. If she (or he) is not satisfied, a brief time-out is called while that person's position and related feelings are expressed again.

The discussion does not proceed until each partner is satisfied that the salient aspects of his position are understood. For example:

Him: I'm out there all day long, getting one turndown after another. Being a salesman is tough. Some days it really gets to me.

Her: Cooking, cleaning, and taking care of the children, that's my day. What the hell are you complaining about?

Him: Hold it. Time out! You passed right over my feelings. Can you please restate what I said from my viewpoint? [He is asking for an empathic response.]

Her: It sounded as if you were trying to make me feel guilty, and I won't have any of that. [Rather than looking at his feelings, she is still focusing on her own.]

Him: That wasn't my intention. I was just feeling a bit frustrated. Do you understand? [He is restating his position and asking her to express *his* position in her own words.]

Her: I understand now. You are feeling frustrated after a day of rejection. Each rejection chips away at you; it's discouraging. What you're saying makes perfect sense, it's just that I had a lousy day, also.

Him: Sounds like you are also pretty frustrated. I can imagine that days filled with cooking, cleaning, and the kids leave you feeling under-stimulated and unfulfilled. Sometimes you feel worn down and impatient.

When they were being empathic, it was as if they were silently asking, "How does he [she] see it? How does he [she] feel? How would I feel if this were said to me?" This is empathy, a critical ingredient in mutually satisfying relationships. It is an effort to understand another's beliefs, practices, and feelings without necessarily sharing or agreeing with them. I call such couples "validators." In the midst of disagreement they still let their partners know that they consider his or her emotions valid, even if they don't agree with them. This expression of mutual respect tends to limit the number of arguments couples have.

In business some people argue that empathy is inappropriate, or too "soft." In fact, empathy in the workplace succeeds extraordinarily well, and those that dismiss it do so because of misunderstanding. They confuse empathy with psychoanalyzing and agreement. Empathy is neither; it is about understanding someone's point of view or perspective. Particularly in business dealings, understanding how someone feels can lead to more skillful negotiations and a win/win resolution.

When individuals in a dispute, for example, realize they are being understood, that the other person sees how the situation seems to them, the statements are likely to grow less exaggerated and defensive. It is also more likely that the attitude "I am one hundred percent right and you are one hundred percent wrong" will be abandoned in favor of attitudes that are softer and more collaborative.

If couples conscientiously practice responding empathetically, even if a time-out is necessary to settle down, it may seem forced and silly at the beginning, but many difficulties not caused by actual differences but by misunderstandings and emotional alienation will be prevented. What's more, when feelings are identified and expressed in an empathic manner, a couple will sometimes find that the real difficulty has little to do with what they are arguing about.

An argument about flirting at social gatherings, for instance, might be only a symptom of two people's assumptions: "If you loved me, you wouldn't do this" or "If you respected me, you'd trust me." The fears behind the assumption are quite similar: "I'm afraid you don't love/respect me."

At this level, seeming differences turn into shared experiences; that is, each partner might feel emotionally threatened by the flirting or the command to stop, and the surface disagreement may be only an expression of the differences in the way each partner avoids or copes with very similar feelings and experiences. Only by being sensitive to each other's feelings will a couple achieve a level of discussion where these discoveries and connective outcomes are more likely to occur.

In the workplace parallel, Dr. William Kahn, a psychologist at Boston University's School of Management, writing in the *Academy of Management Journal* (33, 1990), tells of a manager who was able to turn a situation around with one of her employees by simply being attuned to her feelings and observing her body language.

The manager's empathic response to what she observed turned her employee's frustration into enthusiasm; the encounter ended with humor that tightened the bond between them. Ordinarily, without the skilled empathic response, the outcome would likely have become adversarial.

Nonverbal Messages

Others, whether they are spouses, colleagues, or subordinates, frequently don't tell us everything with their words; instead, they tell us in their tone of voice, facial expression, or in other nonverbal ways. In the workplace and at home, body language can be critically important.

In fact, it is not uncommon for communication to be impeded by confusing the spoken message with contradictory body language, for instance, offering assistance in an accusatory manner, lecturing and moralizing.

Oftentimes, even the statement "we need to talk" takes on an emotional tone and is interpreted ominously: "Uh oh, he [she] wants to complain about me again."

Research indicates that a large percentage of our communication with others is carried out on a nonverbal level. Analysis of slow-motion films of couples in various situations reveals that the two individuals continually "speak" to each other in nonverbal modes (gestures, actions, facial expressions, and the like). When couples are in discord, for example, messages abound without their uttering a word.

Strategic avoidance of eye contact, the utilization of eye rolling and expressions of disgust, the tendency to glare at one's partner, clenched hands, quick movements—all of these are powerful indications of negativity. Stylistic aspects of what is being said are crucial as well. Tone of voice, volume, and pacing all make a difference.

Consider this example: Connie and Sam have been married for two years, they have no children. Connie has just been offered a promotion at her job, with more responsibility and a substantial increase in salary. She will now be making about a third more than Sam. That day when she returns home she meet her husband at the door and bubbles her good news.

Sam, with a long face, says, "Gee, that's wonderful. I'm really glad for you." Connie is puzzled. "You say you're glad but your face doesn't show it. Is something wrong?" Sam folds his arms across his chest and takes a step back. "No, I'm fine," he says in a flat tone. "Are you sure?" Connie asks once again. "You seem like you're not really happy." "I'm happy, damn it!" Sam insists. "I'm happy."

The remainder of the evening is strained. In the morning Sam confesses. "I guess I was jealous," he says softly, looking at Connie and placing his hand on her shoulder. "I have been busting my back trying to get ahead in my job and I haven't received so much as a thank you from my boss. I feel unappreciated. Now you tell me you have been offered a major promotion. It took me back initially. But I thought about it some more last night, and I am happy for you. I really am. It just took me a little time to get myself together. Congratulations!"

Connie smiles at Sam. "Thank you," she says. "Your support means a lot to me."

By revisiting the exchange of the previous evening with a different attitude that is conveyed not only by the honesty of his words, but by the very different physical gestures and tone that support his words, Sam creates a very different outcome.

Behavioral scientists have found that most of us rely on nonverbal behavior in all of our exchanges, but it is particularly telling as a means of communicating attraction or disdain in a social encounter. The face, followed by the hands and feet, are considered sources of the most fertile cues to the meaning of a communication.

For example, if a husband suggests sex to his wife and she says no, the meaning of her response can be clarified by the facial expression that accompanies it. If, as she says no, she smiles, she may be signaling: "Don't just ask, seduce me, be playful." If she frowns and presses her lips together angrily, her refusal is scornful and decisive: "I'm angry. How can you expect me to be intimate after embarrassing me last night!"

If she offers a meek no, exhaling emphatically, as she responds, her decline may be more delay than refusal: "I'm pretty tired now, but perhaps later, or tomorrow." In each instance, the same verbal response was given, but the unspoken accompaniment relayed a very different message.

In the same vein, if a woman asks a man his feelings about her, his response of "I love you" would be greatly strengthened if he maintained eye contact while speaking. Moving his open hands toward her would say something very different than clenching his fists when he answers. And sitting with his knees tightly closed together would express a very different feeling than would his answering her question while reaching toward her with open, outstretched legs.

Related to the nonverbal aspect of a communication is the style of delivery. Consider the simple, factual statement, "I cleared the kitchen table." A partner may say this in a haughty tone of voice that conveys, "Someone had to do it, certainly can't count on you!" or a friendly tone that says, "I'm glad to be able to help out." An intimate may request help cleaning the table in a heavy voice that says, "I'm exhausted, please lend a hand"; a hurt tone that says, "Poor me, you always leave me the dirty work"; or an angry tone that says, "Damn you, I resent having to remind you about cleaning up."

The rhythm of a message—where the emphasis is placed and the pacing—adds another dimension. Even Muriel, a three-year-old child, is sensitive to these undercurrents. Muriel's parents consider themselves civilized; they never fight in front of Muriel. "In fact," they boast, "we rarely even raise our voices in front of her." Yet Muriel senses that Mom and Dad are frequently angry.

"Don't be mad!" she pleads defensively when she tears her new dress. "Dad's not mad, honey. Mom should have saved the dress for a special occasion." Turning to his wife, he says, "I'm sure you can sew that tear, dear."

It seems a simple, even a loving request. The word "dear" is even thrown in. But Muriel hears nothing simple or loving in the statement. She hears the tight anger in her father's voice, his emphasis on "you," the slight but strategic pause before "dear."

On the surface Muriel's parents are communicating that everything is fine; this is a loving, cooperative family. But the manner of speaking, the music of the words, indicate that everything is not fine. Muriel is sensitive to these continual contradictions, and she reacts by developing an apologetic posture in an attempt to relieve her own anxiety and assuage the controlled rage between her parents. Rather than deal with their feelings openly, her parents have become expert in engaging in pseudo openness.

Just as tone, rhythm, and accompanying emotion affect the meaning of a communication, volume also discloses a tremendous amount about an interaction. Volume often drops off, perhaps even to a whisper, under certain circumstances. A lowered voice may convey caring, as when we comfort the bereaved; intimacy, by signaling, "What I have to say is for your ears alone"; the quiet before the storm, when the lowered volume is accompanied by slow, painstakingly deliberate speech through clenched teeth; or fear, as in "Don't attack me. I am lowering my voice to demonstrate my defenselessness."

Of course, as with other stylistic and nonverbal aspects of relating, meaning may vary depending on culture and background.

In one family soft, melodic speech with only minor animation is associated with calm, loving messages. In another family, the voice and energy level are higher. Family members yell continually, orchestrating their speech with flailing arms. In this family, these are the signals of love and warmth.

Getting to the Point

Not only is it important that the content of a statement be consistent with other factors in the delivery, messages are also best communicated directly.

Janet and Dan have been married three years. They were both married before. When Dan was still married to his first wife, he had an affair with Janet, who was divorced. Although Dan and Janet were both affected by their brief encounter (it happened during one of Dan's business trips), it was not pursued at the time because of Dan's marriage. Two months later, Dan's wife left him for another man. Six months after that, Dan and Janet were married. Because he slept with her while he was still married to his first wife, Janet worries that Dan will have affairs while married to her. She is secretly suspicious of him.

Dan regards his infidelity in his previous marriage as an exception to his usual behavior, and views the motivation behind it as desperation. His marriage had been deteriorating for a long time, and he acted quite out of his character. He operates from a standpoint of fidelity and trust with Janet. She, in turn, is guided by mistrust and her suspicious attitude: "If he did it to his previous wife, he will probably do it to me." Consequently, their discussions about absences from home, particularly business trips, are filled with misunderstanding:

> **Janet:** You know what, I think I'll go to Chicago with you, maybe I can be of some help to you there.
> **Dan:** That's okay, Jan. I'm provided with a nice hotel room, meals, transportation, and so on. I don't really need any help.
> **Janet:** *(disappointed)* Oh, then I can keep you company.
> **Dan:** *(starting to experience a vague sense of guilt)* Jan, it's nice of you to want to be with me, but my schedule keeps me busy from nine in the morning to midnight. Since it wouldn't be appropriate for you to sit in on business meetings, I would hardly see you.
> **Janet:** *(persistent, with a trace of annoyance in her voice)* I think I'd like to go anyway.
> **Dan:** *(with impatience and annoyance)* Listen, the company won't pay your way, and I would hardly see you, so there's no point in our spending an extra five hundred dollars that we can ill afford for nothing. Let's leave it at that.
> **Janet:** Let's not leave it at that. I'm going!
> **Dan:** *(angrily and with frustration)* Shit! Janet, for Christ's sake, when you get so damned unreasonable, I feel as if I don't know you anymore. You're not like the woman I married.
> **Janet:** *(her anxiety and resentment escalating)* That's it! You don't want to be with me anymore. I knew it! You're looking for someone else.

Conversations based on indirectness and private, untested assumptions such as Janet's and Dan's are frequently disastrous. In this instance, Dan assumes Janet is merely being pigheaded. Janet, of course, assumes Dan, cornered, is purposely evasive. Had she directly stated her concern or had Dan asked why the trip was so important, the outcome might have been different.

It is probable that these patterns of behavior are somewhat present in almost all relationships. There is an argument whose source is unclear or camouflaged. The result after many futile bouts is often of the you-hurt-me-so-I'll-hurt-you variety; and, in many instances, vindictiveness becomes the major force in the gradual weakening of the relationship.

As the negativity created by indirectness escalates, it spills over into other areas of the relationship; that is, once a negative, destructive atmosphere of misunderstanding has been established, more indirectness and misunderstanding are likely to follow as protection against the "enemy." For example, Janet may begin to attack Dan on any number of insignificant issues: his dress, his manners, his parenting, and so on.

In actuality, Janet's criticisms are related to something entirely different: She is insecure and afraid of losing Dan. Stating her real concern in the attack-counterattack atmosphere of her own making, however, would leave her feeling vulnerable. Instead, she is caught in a series of relationship-defeating attempts to allay her anxiety while avoiding a straightforward discussion of her concern.

In marriage therapy, as Dr. Paul Watzlawick and his associates describe in their book *Change,* one frequently sees both spouses caught in a futile push-pull based on indirectly expressed speculations. For instance, a wife may have the impression that her husband is not open enough for her to know where she stands with him, what is going on in his head, what he is doing when he is away from home, and so on.

Quite naturally, she will therefore attempt to make herself more secure by asking him questions, watching his behavior, and checking on him in a variety of other ways. He is likely to consider her behavior intrusive and react by withholding information that in and of itself would be quite harmless and irrelevant, "just to teach her that I am not a child in need of checking."

Rather than making her back down, her husband's reaction increases her insecurity and provides further fuel for her worries and her distrust: "If he does not talk to me about even these little things, he *must* be hiding something." The less information he gives her, the more persistently will she seek it; and the more she seeks it, the less he will give her.

It is not long before the drama evolves to a point that Dr. Watzlawick views as reminiscent of two sailors hanging out of either side of a sailboat in order to steady it: The more one leans overboard, the more the other has to hang out to compensate for the instability created by the other's attempts at stabilizing the boat, while the boat itself would be quite steady if not for the insecurities of its passengers.

It is predictable that unless something changes in this situation—the couple discusses their assumptions openly and explicitly—the occupants of the boat-marriage will be under constant unnecessary strain or, worse yet, finish up in the water. A direct and pointed statement by one of the partners may not, in fact, resolve a relationship issue. It may result in an admission that indeed there is a problem—and that's a good start.

The essential factor is that a clear exchange where the message sent is the message received provides the means for discussion. The couple may even conclude that they are at a temporary impasse; that is, they may agree that they disagree on some issue. This recognition, although it may seem limited, is a start. It is preferable to the undercurrent of torment and nagging uncertainty that accompanies obfuscation.

Yet another variation of indirectness that fosters ill will and confusion is the disguised request. A couple has just come out of the water after a delightful moonlit swim. The woman says, "Let's go inside. I'm sleepy." The man responds, "It's nice out here. Why don't we lie and rest here?" The woman, angry, storms into the house. The man, equally angry, drives off to a local bar.

What happened? She, by saying she was "sleepy," was actually signaling her desire to make love in the house. He, ironically, was signaling his desire to make love in the moonlight. Neither directly said what he or she wanted, and each felt rejected by the other. The evening ended in anger and hurt rather than in pleasure. Preventing this unfortunate turn of events may have been as simple as saying, "Let's go inside. I'm in the mood to make love" or "It's nice out here. Why don't we make love in the moonlight?"

Many requests are not expressed openly and directly. Often we don't want to take responsibility for our requests, so we hide and disguise them in questions, hints, obscure suggestions, and countless other manipulations, all in an effort to satisfy our desires without the risk of being rejected.

Open requests require an awareness of our desires and involve several risks: (1) an acknowledgment that the other person has something to offer that is of value. This recognition poses a particular threat to couples engaged in a power struggle. By asking for less or asking in a disguised form, the asker "discounts" the spouse's power; (2) being asked to reciprocate. Doubting one's willingness or capacity to satisfy the other's requests, one may prefer to stay self-contained rather than being reciprocal; (3) rejection. Many of us have a fear of the word "no"; and, by being vague, we hope to temper the pain of refusal.

The problem with requests, as with all indirect messages, is that those that are not understood are less likely to be satisfied. What's more, resentment often accompanies the unmet desire and is expressed in disguised form through nagging, criticism and other kinds of annoyances and frustrations. Ultimately, the opportunity for a compromise, or at least some understanding of the refusal, is lost.

Tool Kit

Here is a potpourri of guidelines for communicating more effectively:

1. In this experience with nonverbal communication, the goal is to highlight inconsistencies in what the message receiver *hears* and what he or she *sees* expressed through body language. Each partner will alternate expressing a sentiment and canceling its meaning with a gesture, grimace, motion, facial expression, or some other nonverbal behavior. The sentiments, expressed in your own words, should include: (1) an expression of approval. For example, as Jill compliments Mark on a decision he has made, she looks down, shakes her head side to side and plants her hands on her hips: all actions that signal disapproval and resignation to Mark; (2) a caring expression. For example, saying something supportive while grimacing; and (3) an expression of availability Problem solve, help with chores, do a favor, honor a request—perhaps with a posture of resignation and impatience. Be aware of how you feel as you send and receive these inconsistent messages. Discuss exactly what you and your partner do to cancel the verbal messages. Do any of these ways of canceling feel familiar? After completing the discussion, change the body language and express approval, caring, and availability again. This time match the spoken word with the unspoken signals. Discuss the difference. On a daily basis be alert to the unspoken cues of your spouse that express approval, caring, and availability.
2. About feelings: No matter how discouraging your past has been or how restricting your upbringing, there is plenty of basis for a rich love life if you can learn to accept your feelings. To be open you need to understand what you feel, know where that feeling comes from, and be able to express that feeling. If you get stuck ask yourself: What am I afraid of losing? How may I be hurt? Am I afraid of accepting some part of myself? As you ask these questions of yourself you will find, over time, that you can answer them more easily. You will become more aware of your feelings and

get through the impasse. If you exercise muscles they become toned and respond more effectively; in similar fashion, if your feelings begin to be acknowledged and expressed more freely they, too, will respond naturally. In those instances when you are unable to identify your feelings at the moment that you are discussing something with your partner, continue to think about it after your discussion. If you come up with afterthoughts, share them with your partner. Later is better than never. It goes something like this, "Remember yesterday when we were talking about..."

3. When something is wanted—be it change, clarification, reassurance, companionship, or support—it is important that the message be direct and to the point. Speaking in generalities will not get the message across. Here is an experience to strengthen direct communication. It is designed to be completed while you and your partner are sitting face to face. It is very important to maintain eye contact throughout. Making some kind of physical contact as well is likely to deepen the involvement and increase the probability of learning something about your partner, yourself, and how you interact. For about five minutes, alternate saying sentences to each other that begin with the words "I assume." Fill in the sentence with assumptions about your partner (e.g., "I assume you hate visiting my parents"); yourself ("I assume you know how critically important a promotion is to me"); or the relationship ("I assume you are pleased with our sexual experiences"). Don't discuss the assumptions; simply alternate making statements beginning with "I assume." If you get stuck, stay with it. Repeat the beginning of the sentence and see what words come to you. After five minutes or so, discuss what each of you experienced and check out your assumptions. What did you discover about your own and your partner's assumptions? To what extent were your assumptions refuted? Which of those are you willing to revise? Take some time to discuss these issues with your partner.

4. In what manner do you normally make requests of each other? Are they straightforward or indirect, such as "You don't want to go to the store for me, do you? If only I had time to get there myself." "Are you expecting to be busy all day today?" What's the basis for your disguised requests? Take a few minutes to discuss these issues with your partner. Follow up this exercise with an actual request. Note the wording being suggested for making requests: (1) begin with "I"; (2) be specific; and (3) use "want" (desire, prefer, like) rather than "need." A want is something that is desired but not necessary. "Need" implies that something is critical to survival,

which is hardly ever the case in request making. In addition to the appropriate phrasing for the request, consider the timing. Try to select a time when the probability of success is high. Do not make a request when your partner is obviously busy, tired, or otherwise out-of-sorts. If your partner's cues as to availability are ambiguous, ask for clarification.

Discussion Forum

Initiate a discussion of importance to the relationship. You may discuss division of marital/parental responsibilities, in-laws, feelings about a recent issue, some aspect of the intimacy between you, or any other topic of mutual interest. As you do this, focus your attention exclusively on what your partner is saying and see things from their perspective. Quiet that inner voice that may be preparing a rebuttal. In effect, dig down and put yourself completely in your partner's shoes, and experience what he or she is saying as if it were you. Bring your focus primarily to the feelings, but attend to the emphasis, tone, rhythm, facial expression, body posture, etc.

When your partner is finished (limit the time to ten minutes) summarize what your partner has said, providing the deepest and most thorough understanding that you can muster. When you have done this, discuss how it feels to be so thoroughly understood and develop a plan for continuing the experience.

• Empathizing will strengthen my relationship.

STRATEGY SIX
■■■■■■■■■■
Build on Strengths

Whose Vision?

Today, almost everyone has heard of a separation that appears to be a sudden and unexpected occurance in a seemingly tranquil relationship. Of course, this is rarely the case; and a closer look at these relationships reveals not fulfillment marred by a crisis, but a profound and cancerous unhappiness resembling that of the characters in Elia Kazan's novel *The Arrangement*.

In that story, the protagonist has become increasingly (but quietly) dissatisfied with his marriage, and at age forty-three he engages in a serious affair with a younger woman. He is confused by his own behavior and feels guilty because he either doesn't understand or won't acknowledge that his wife's good nature is leaving him unfulfilled and conflicted.

His wife, true to her helping nature, arranges a plan, a different "style of life" for the two of them, with the hope that it will draw them together and rid her husband of his misery. The husband complies, whether out of passivity or sheer exhaustion, and for almost a year they live in a way designed to protect the couple (him!) from the conflicts that threaten their illusory togetherness. The arrangement, appropriately called "the fortress," because it disallows any expression of discontent, backfires: Instead of eliminating the husband's marital discontent, it causes him to become even more passive and finally, unable to respond sexually.

During the eleven-month fortress period, the husband and wife are the envy of their few friends. The husband's apparent receptiveness projects an image of sharing, togetherness, and unusual devotion. Below the surface, however, is a serious dilemma, for the dream of happily ever after is not shared; it belongs only to the wife. A near-fatal auto accident, which is recognized by the husband as a suicide gesture, forcefully shatters the fantasy. The husband, after his recovery, leaves his wife.

Perhaps with less drama but through an essentially similar process—avoiding or handling differences ineffectively—many couples grow apart. Although they appear to share common goals, their "arrangement" is based on one person's vision. The other is silently veering off in another direction.

Dealing with differences openly and working toward resolution can be forces that prevent the buildup of a fortress. In contrast, failing to resolve differences or resolving them at the cost of emotional casualties puts you on the road to marital misery.

If there's one lesson I've learned in my years of writing about and treating couples, it is that a lasting marriage absolutely requires the ability to resolve the conflicts that are inevitable in any relationship. You don't have to be sitting in a business meeting to be involved in negotiation; you may discuss decisions as simple as where to go to dinner with your spouse, or what to watch on TV with your family.

Confirmation of the importance of conflict resolution was found in a study of twenty marriages lasting twenty-five years or more. Dr. Florence Kaslow, director of the Florida Couple and Family Institute, identified what distinguishes those couples most satisfied with their relationship. The major factor contributing to satisfaction was joint problem-solving ability, mentioned by 70 percent of both highly satisfied and mildly satisfied couples.

Indeed, it turns up in virtually every long-term study of marriage. It is what enables couples to navigate the obstacles of relationships. Howard Markman, Ph.D., professor of psychology and head of the Center for Marital and Family Studies at the University of Denver, calls it "constructive arguing" and also finds it to be the single biggest predictor of marital success over time.

It is also an excellent predictor in the business world. In a survey of retail buyers in department store chains, each of whom handled merchandise worth $15 million to $30 million, the style of conflict resolution was an accurate barometer of the manufacturer-retailer relationship. When conflict resolution was aggressive, characterized by threats and demands, it was poor; when compromise ruled, the workability of the relationship increased.

For some couples who are unsuccessful in their efforts, the "solution" to unresolved conflict is a double life: an emotional divorce from one's partner (preserving the convenience of family life), along with a search for emotional union outside the relationship. The "other man" or "other woman" is sought as a diversion to make a dreary relationship tolerable. The relief is merely temporary and resolves nothing.

Other couples react to their emotional divorce by establishing a pseudo-relationship; "a fortress" wherein the satisfaction derived from outside activities masks the emptiness within. Frequent entertaining and extravagant dining out, frequent residence changing, elaborate decorating, and job-hopping can be attempts by the couple to fill the void.

Still others engage in major battles during which nothing gets settled, and both partners are left emotionally and sometimes physically bruised. Many relationship battles zigzag through an obstacle course of withdrawal, denial, subterfuge, and out-of-control full-scale attacks. Typically these battles take on the characteristics of war, the intention being to win and bring down the "enemy."

Victory is achieved through destruction. Consequently, "winning" in a marital conflict is an illusion. It is an empty victory because it encourages deception in future disagreements ("I'm not about to let him use this against me"), fosters pessimism ("What's the use, I can never get my point across, this relationship will never work"), and will very likely lead to retaliation to "even the score."

In some war-like battles, after many disturbing fights, partners may even give up hope of any individual gain and focus instead on limiting the other's advantage. Rather than anything being settled, disagreements are instigated to torture the other partner.

Sometimes the torture is self-inflicted. One of the executives I lunched with told me of an experience he had some years ago. He and a colleague were both refused a promotion. They both took it badly, but the executive I was speaking with settled himself down, had a talk with his boss, kept an open mind, and learned what he needed to do in order to bring his talents more fully to the organization. He was eventually promoted. His colleague complained to anyone who would listen, went on a drinking binge, became disrespectful to the boss, and was fired.

Where's the Beef?

While some couples live in denial and others are battle-worn from the futile wars they wage, still others are not even clear what the real issues are. The problems may be suppressed, camouflaged, or put forth abruptly, defensively, vaguely, in the form of a lecture or with substantial hostility. It is as if the kitchen is on fire and they are pouring water on the hallway.

On the surface, clearly defining the issues sounds absurdly easy, and for some people it is. For many, though, going beyond the basics—he frequently leaves clothes lying around; she forgets to gas up the car; he hogs the newspaper; she monopolizes conversations—isn't as easy as it seems.

It is not uncommon to find that the focus is given to an insignificant issue, while the actual problem is related to something entirely different. For example, Alex berates Florence for being a mediocre housekeeper even though the housekeeping is only a mild irritant at most, because he is jealous of how well she is doing in her career while his is floundering.

Alex's struggle to climb the corporate ladder and increase his income has been less than spectacular, and he knows that if he attacked Florence's stunning success it would expose his own feelings of inadequacy and envy. In order to avoid this painful self-disclosure, he chooses (perhaps without being aware of it) to pick on something safe for him, Florence's housekeeping. In effect, he is saying, "See, you aren't so terrific after all," without having to risk revealing himself.

It is unreasonable to insist that a woman who puts in a thirteen-hour day at the office come home and transform into "wonder wife." And yet, redistributing roles and responsibilities in a family is often not as straightforward as saying, "You take out the garbage, I'll sweep the floor." It often gets down to people's core beliefs about who they are and what they need to be doing to feel good about themselves. The reactions people have to such things are often distressingly irrational—even to themselves!

My interviews with execs revealed that ironically, once a wife's income is actually greater than her husband's, he tends to be less involved at home, while she is more likely to increase her home-based responsibilities. Some men need to feel that they are still the head of the household to feel like a man, and some women, uncomfortable with their success, compensate by trying to be all things to everybody.

While this arrangement may project a facade of harmony, it is not a lasting solution. Often, as with Alex and Florence, the issues are buried in surface complaints. In the case of Alex and Florence, we were able to get beyond the unimportant issue and agree on some understandings that worked very well for them.

First and foremost, they agreed to keep talking about the issue and not camouflage or avoid it. Alex and Florence, like many couples today, are inventing a family life that is radically different from those they knew growing up. These kinds of issues don't get solved in a single conversation. Nor can any of us assume that the distribution of household chores, money, and decision-making power will just work itself out on its own. These issues are fraught with emotion for most of us, and certainly were for Alex and Florence. Each partner is consciously dealing with old role models, their own and their parents' expectations for what it means to be successful.

After some discussion, they recognized that the most important attitude for a couple to maintain in this situation is that they are in it *together*. Like a business problem, their issues must be defined clearly. In this instance, the problem is trying to manage the crushing load of two jobs, two kids, and a mountain of laundry. The problem is *not* who is making what salary. That is a distraction from the real task: Working together to figure out what needs to get done each week to keep the children safe and happy and the household orderly and running smoothly.

As for decisions about money, Alex and Florence took the time to outline a policy to determine who makes the monetary decisions. They addressed important questions such as How are bills to be paid? What kinds of decisions are left up to the individual and which need to be discussed by both of us?

Lastly, they acknowledged that their issues about money and power are old and deep. They agreed to seek help if they found themselves getting into repeated and heated arguments about money, decision-making, and household tasks.

Pulling Back the Curtain

Alex and Florence are certainly not the only couple struggling to define their problems. All couples are prone to camouflage a variety of issues some of the time, and often work hard to do so.

A couple going out, for example, may disagree on the directions to their destination. It begins with a simple question that barely makes a blip on the conflict radar screen—"Shouldn't you have made a left there?"—and soon they are arguing as if their very lives depended on being correct. Neither will let up, and neither will concede. Is the impassioned arguing really about the possibility of making a wrong turn? Hardly. But identifying the *real* issues is no easy matter.

Consider Mr. and Mrs. Smith, a couple who argue regularly about his coming to dinner on time. Mrs. Smith, a full-time homemaker, describes the problem quite simply: "My husband is always late for dinner. That's all there is to it." Prompted to discuss the specific sequence of events prior to the dinner hour, Mrs. Smith provided more detail.

At six o'clock, when my husband arrives home, I am in the kitchen putting the finishing touches on dinner. At six-fifteen, after washing up and changing his clothes, my husband brings me a whiskey sour and a beer for himself, and we take ten minutes out for a drink. There is usually some pleasant talk of the day's happenings, and my husband usually gets himself another beer. Typically, I suggest he give me a hand in the kitchen rather than finishing his second drink alone. And, typically, he grumbles about my suggestion while I go back into the kitchen muttering some angry words about equality and all that stuff.

Then comes six-forty-five. Dinner's ready and on the table. I call once, no answer. Twice. "Yeah, I'm coming." Five minutes later I go into the TV room enraged and tell him that dinner's cold and he's an inconsiderate bastard.

Now he comes. We eat in silence, we don't even exchange glances. After dinner we soften, he even helps with the dishes occasionally. That is our dinner routine.

Looking at the more detailed pattern, it is evident the problem involves more than remedying a simple case of tardiness. Mrs. Smith acknowledges that beckoning her husband repeatedly doesn't work, yet she plays her part in the dinnertime drama in exactly the same manner each evening.

How is it that Mrs. Smith doesn't tire of being rejected in her bid for help? And couldn't Mrs. Smith call her husband several minutes before dinner was ready? Certainly, this seems an obvious solution. How did she miss it? Is there some sort of payoff Mr. and Mrs. Smith derive from their behavior?

After scrutinizing her actions, Mrs. Smith realizes that, in fact, she does not want her husband's help in the kitchen even though she requests it on cue each evening. This becomes apparent when Mrs. Smith asks herself what she wants her husband to do in the kitchen. In actuality, she would rather do everything herself. By asking her husband to help out, Mrs. Smith is really fishing for a statement of appreciation for her *own* efforts. Reluctantly, Mrs. Smith, unhappy in her role as homemaker, also recognizes that her husband's rejection affords her the opportunity to feel superior by badgering him about his uncooperativeness.

While his wife bemoans her fate, Mr. Smith expresses his resentment and wrestles out of his inferior position through noncompliance: "Let her call me, it serves her right for asking me to help after a hard day's work. I'll show her who's in charge here." The dinnertime dilemma is now redefined. Mrs. Smith wants to feel appreciated and respected, Mr. Smith wants the same. The evening meal simply became a convenient—and misleading—arena.

Some couples report a pattern of fights that break out over something quite obviously trivial after their lovemaking was particularly satisfying and connective. These couples keep love at bay to avoid the feeling of engulfment. Typically, this is an adult who, as a child, was not allowed to satisfy a natural need for independence and now mistrusts anything (like closeness) that hints at restraint.

It works this way: One partner complains about the other's annoying habit, or some minor frustration gives rise to a disproportionate reaction, or the kids are too noisy and a volley of accusations result. The catalyst could be any number of imperfections in their living arrangements, and there is no dearth of these to complain about for people whose lives are intertwined.

In any case, one person gets furious, and the other one is provoked and becomes enraged. In a flash harsh words are exchanged and the recent lovemaking seems like a distant memory.

That is just the point. Some fights have no issue except "Keep your distance!" It is reminiscent of a porcupine metaphor. Two porcupines are huddled together on a cold winter's night. As the temperature drops, the animals move closer together. But then there is a problem; each keeps getting pricked by the other's quills. Finally, with much shifting and shuffling and changing positions, they manage to work out an equilibrium whereby each gets maximum warmth with a minimum of painful pricking from the other.

Many couples have something in common with the huddling porcupines. They want to achieve and maintain a kind of equilibrium: warmth and closeness but without the sometimes agonizing "pricking" that comes from continuous interaction with another human being. The problem is that, unlike the porcupines, the shifting and shuffling done by couples can lead one or both to feel emotionally unsafe. Couples who feel unsafe in that manner generally shield their vulnerability and shut down, resulting in a relationship that lacks energy and vibrancy.

If the couple has children, they present another opportunity for obscuring the real issue. A wife says to her husband, "I don't like the way you exclude our son from your activities. I feel like he's growing up without your influence." The real issue not being addressed is: "I feel neglected as well, and I am upset that you are so involved with your own activities that you spend too little time with me."

A wife says to her husband, "You are too easygoing with the children; you are going to make it harder for them to adjust to the real world." The real issue not being addressed is: "I feel as if you are the children's favorite, and I am jealous that they seem to love you more than they love me."

Lastly, most of us are prone to hide what we want behind the guise of right vs. wrong. This is an underlying attitude that, if held, stymies even the best intentions of couples that are struggling with discord. Proclamations of right and wrong are usually arbitrary rules that an individual assigns to his or her preferences.

A man, for example, is lying on the couch on a Sunday afternoon watching the football game. His partner attacks him: "How can you lie there all day! Only an idiot would spend his Sunday in front of the TV." The man rushes to his defense: "This is my only chance to relax! Look who's talking anyway, you with your ridiculous craft projects!"

The implication here is that there is something the matter with the man, that he is doing something wrong, something he should feel guilty about. His response is, in effect, "I'm okay, and there's something wrong with you." The wrong-begets-wrong cycle is likely to escalate as both parties become further entrenched in their own truth. Thus, the discussion becomes adversarial and fixed on who's right and who's wrong and misses the point completely.

In actuality, the issue, as with most, is based less on right and wrong than on preference: "I like/ I don't like; I want/ I don't want." In this instance, the wife wanted to spend some time with her husband on a Sunday afternoon, and instead of stating that directly, she protected her feelings from rejection by attacking him instead. She hoped that by using her "there's something wrong with you" message, she could provoke him into shutting the TV and paying attention to her without having to reveal her desire and possibly risking rejection.

It is apparent that love partners who find themselves fighting about things that seem not worth the effort, not occasionally, but regularly, have a hidden agenda; they have designed the fight to indirectly get revenge, are projecting their own issues, being manipulative, or unconsciously creating distance.

In other words, while all couples fight, at least occasionally, it is very easy to fight about blurred issues. The real issues remain untouched while the emotions roar and the words fly, all in the wrong direction. Here are several suggestions for the good fight, or better yet, a discussion that isn't overshadowed by emotion:

1. If your partner has accused you of being defensive, or if you realize that about yourself, make an effort to agree in principle with what your partner has said. Don't do this as a diversionary tactic; do it with sincerity. For example, if your partner says you are selfish, respond with something like, "you're right, I am selfish on occasion." Debating about whether you were selfish in any particular instance will probably result in a futile argument, but agreeing that you are, at times, selfish (which is probably true!), will help you sidestep an adversarial brawl.
2. Since not being defensive is very important, here is another approach to consider—practice being responsive. When you are responsive, you are aware of your feelings but don't let them control you. This is extremely empowering; it involves being open to views that are in conflict with yours. In talking to your partner, for example, instead of arguing ferociously or explaining yourself frantically, you might simply listen carefully without interrupting (interrupting is a dead giveaway that you are being defensive) and say something like, "I understand what you are saying, your view is credible, but I see it differently." Or, rather than reacting emotionally, you might say, "I am viewing things differently, let me think about it a bit and then we'll discuss it."
3. Recall that every issue is an interaction between *two* people. For example, there can be no dominating husband without a submissive wife, no interrupting wife without a passive and willing husband. Every "villain" requires a cooperative "victim." Consequently, when discussing a problem, it is good policy to state your *own* role in the issue rather than focusing on your partner's. If you are interested in promoting resolution, it is best to start with yourself. As Daniel Goleman reports in *Working with Emotional Intelligence*, "At American Express, the ability to spot potential sources of conflict, take responsibility for one's own role, apologize if need be, and engage openly in a discussion of each person's perspective is prized in their financial advisors."
4. Review the themes of your conflicts. During a time when conflict is not raging, you can do this with your partner. What underlying issue connects all or most of your arguments? Think about this until you find

some commonality because, in fact, there is practically always a connection. Most of us have one theme underlying all the fights throughout our marriage that plays out with endless variations. Puzzle out the theme and you'll have a handle on all of your fights. For instance, a couple may have what appears to be a host of unrelated arguments when in fact all involve one person trying to exert control over the other.

Action Plan

When an atmosphere of trust and goodwill is developing and communication is becoming more effective so that issues are clearly defined, partners are in a good position to bargain, negotiate, and work at compromises in their relationship. To some people, "bargaining" and "negotiating" are terms to be applied to business, not relationships. I disagree.

While everyone who works in an organization needs these abilities, and those who can negotiate most skillfully are vital, the same applies to couple relationships. Most people have different tastes, attitudes, behaviors, and goals, and these differences can be resolved only on the basis of mutually understood rules of exchange.

Charles and Joan, a couple in their late twenties, operate within the framework of what might be described as a "traditional" marriage. Joan is considerate of and expresses her affection for Charles, takes primary responsibility for the children, prepares meals, and cleans the house. When asked why she does these things, Joan replies, "Because I love Charles."

Joan may indeed love Charles, but she engages in these behaviors in exchange for certain behaviors from Charles. He is considerate of her and expresses his affection for her; he provides their income, makes household repairs, and takes care of the cars. If these behaviors were to stop, would there be a change in Joan's behavior? Quite likely.

Very rarely are individuals so complementary in tastes and desires that negotiating and compromising are not required. Conflict is inevitable unless we have a good understanding of what our partners expect to get and give in return. When this understanding is lacking or the giving and getting cease to be reciprocal, bitterness, resentment, and general unhappiness usually result.

Morris and Evelyn have been married for four years. For the first three years of their marriage, they both worked—Morris as a sales manager for one of the major airlines, Evelyn as a teacher. During those three years, Morris and Evelyn shared a common goal, purchasing a home, which they accomplished. At the end of their third year of marriage, two things happened: Evelyn gave birth, and Morris received a substantial promotion.

As a result of these events, Morris and Evelyn experienced a dramatic change in their usual routine. Evelyn left her teaching position and was at home all day caring for her child. Morris was home less because of his increased responsibility. When Morris returned home, he was sometimes irritable and fatigued. Often, he was greeted by a wife who felt equally off-color.

To prepare himself for the unpleasant news about Evelyn's day and the growing friction at home, Morris began stopping for a drink after work. Evelyn, disgusted with the unpredictability of his arrival home, stopped preparing meals. Morris, in turn, began eating out more frequently. As a result, they become more and more distant. We spoke about it:

Morris: It used to be that we sat down, had cocktails and a leisurely meal together. We would discuss our day and enjoy each other's company. Then I came home and the house was a mess, the meal was lousy, and I was greeted by a tiger ready to lunge at me.

Evelyn: I felt Morris no longer had any interest in me. He seemed to have more interest in his business. When he came home, all he wanted to do was eat quickly, watch TV, and go to sleep. When I suggested that we go out together after the baby went to sleep, he constantly refused because he was tired. Well, I was tired also, but I desperately needed some stimulation.

Morris: We seemed to have lost our synchrony. For example, with sex, Evelyn felt that I was interested only when I was horny, and unresponsive to her needs when she felt sexy. As a result, we hardly had sex anymore.

Both Evelyn and Morris feel they aren't getting an adequate return for their efforts. Morris feels that his difficulties in coping with the pressures of his new position aren't appreciated. Evelyn feels that Morris does not recognize the difficulties of her adjustment. Day after day, night after night, both Evelyn and Morris seek to exert power over each other, to reap his or her fair share.

Fortunately, having a sound relationship and the basis for good communication, they eventually see the futility of their struggle and agree to work things out through compromise. Their attitudes after sitting down together can be characterized thusly: "I can't have everything I want and you can't have everything you want, so let's compromise in such a manner that we each have those things that are most important, and at the same time let us each try to strengthen the other's well-being to the maximum extent possible."

Most couples are either unaware of such a workable "exchange attitude" or merely pay it lip service. As a result, their many differences with regard to food preferences, moods, sex, types of entertainment, choice of friends, responsibility for household tasks, personal habits (e.g., smoking and drinking), and employed activity (e.g., working late or on weekends) are a constant source of friction. The message they convey to each other seems to be "If you won't change for me, then I won't change for you."

In contrast, those couples who live by the tenets of mutual exchange—compromise, recognition of individuality, and compassion—are more likely to discuss conflicting differences and conflicting issues not as adversaries but as partners, and thus avoid endless unnecessary bickering. The message they convey to each other seems to be "You scratch my back and I'll scratch yours." Their goal is to create a *win/win* solution.

Is it worth going to the movie only *you* want to see if it creates feelings of frustration and resentment in your partner? Is it worth getting the price you demand from a supplier if it will impede business deals in the future? Pursuing an I win/you lose strategy means risking damage to your relationship with the other party. In general, an everybody-wins philosophy creates longer-lasting and more successful outcomes than a winner-takes-all approach.

Indeed, as Harvard psychologist Herbert Kelman, who specializes in negotiations, points out in the journal *International Negotiation* (1, 1996), the process of negotiation itself restores cooperation between conflicting parties.

Here are some of the agreements Evelyn and Morris worked out with me: Evelyn agrees not to close in on Morris as soon as he arrives home but to allow him time to shower and take a short nap. Evelyn arranges for a babysitter and is also able to nap and refresh herself in the early evening. They both agree to eat a late dinner together after the baby is asleep. One night a week is set aside for going out for dinner and entertainment.

During their discussions, Morris recognizes that Evelyn's moods and behaviors are greatly influenced by his acknowledging her as a capable homemaker and desirable wife, and that this acknowledgment needs to go beyond the form of a mere statement made to himself. To be most effective, Morris should offer a personal demonstration that he loves and admires her as a person, and that she is as important to him as his work.

Morris's plan includes two elements: expressing his appreciation of Evelyn more often and increasing his involvements in household responsibilities, including sitting down with Evelyn and working out strategies for making life easier.

Morris also suggests to Evelyn that if their relationship does not improve as a result of the numerous exchange agreements, he will consider changing to a less demanding job. Evelyn is profoundly touched by Morris's offer. She recognizes the significance of his statement and tells him so. She adds that his interest and appreciation makes her work more acceptable and a job change is unnecessary. She also begins to express more interest in his work.

The key concepts are *fairness* and *flexibility*—and these, as with all of the principles herein, are directly applicable to the workplace. When a project doesn't go as planned, or takes an unexpected turn, if you act with a sense of fairness and flexibility, you will have the advantage by altering your strategies to deal with unforeseen circumstances. And in a weak economy, workers who can adapt to change while remaining team players are more valuable.

Whenever applicable, a disagreement or conflict with some aspect of your partner's behavior should be approached by offering to change some aspect of your own behavior. Mutuality is more effective than unilateral change attempts because most of us find changing more acceptable if we aren't doing it alone. In addition, one partner's change (Evelyn's agreement to give Morris some private time when he arrives home) makes it easier for the other partner to change (Morris's agreement to give up his after-work stopovers for a drink).

Sometimes, the mutuality may be in the form of one partner offering him- or herself in the service of the other partner's change efforts. This is illustrated by Morris's offer to sit down with Evelyn in an effort to work out strategies for household management. Contrast this with the partner who chronically complains about a messy house and lousy meals but never puts forth a constructive suggestion for remedying the displeasure.

There are several types of negotiating and compromising situations. One is "meeting in the middle ground": being reconciled to buying a medium-priced car rather than either the expensive sports car or the economy compact, or agreeing that one partner will limit his or her drinking to one per evening when the drinking partner would like three drinks an evening and the other prefers that he or she not drink at all.

A second type of compromise involves trading: Alice is paying the bills in return for Tom's keeping the cars maintained.

Another type of negotiating is one that is not immediately time sensitive. In this instance, the couple recognizes that if one spouse does something for the other, the benefited spouse need not *immediately* turn around and pay off the debt. It is assumed on good faith that there will be an opportunity for reciprocity in the future.

One couple, Lois and Ron, faced the problem of a career conflict. Ron is an engineer, Lois is an attorney specializing in corporate law. They both have jobs in Boston and are simultaneously offered new positions, Lois in Chicago, Ron in Dallas. In both cases, the new jobs appear to be just what they are looking for individually. But if they are to continue their relationship, one of them will obviously have to defer to the other's needs.

The position offered Lois gives her an opportunity that simply cannot be duplicated anywhere else in the country. And while Ron's job offer is an extremely good one, there exist a number of other engineering firms doing similar work, two of which are in the Chicago area. So, after discussing the options open to each of them, Ron concedes that his opportunities are more flexible in Chicago than Lois's are in Dallas. He agrees to go to Chicago, where Lois can begin her exciting opportunity.

Within six weeks of their arrival in Chicago, Ron finds a job that is the equivalent of the one he was offered in Dallas. This kind of arrangement, based on the assumption that if there comes a time in their lives when their positions are reversed, the other partner will likewise compromise, is ideal. As with most idealistic promises, though, it works best under good conditions: well-functioning relationships involving a high degree of trust and reciprocity.

When one spouse continues to imply or promise that he or she will do something in the future but never gets around to it, or when one person has an extremely selective memory and recalls all his or her contributions but none of the partner's, relationship discord and bitterness are the predictable outcome.

Whenever differences occur, whether between intimates, business partners, or nations, they are resolved in one of three ways: one party attempts domination (result: hostility, war); there is mutual or unilateral withdrawal (result: divorce, isolation); there is mutual compromise (result: exchange, goodwill). If individuals are seeking a more satisfying relationship with each other rather than divorce or aggression, mutual exchange and compromise clearly offer the greatest promise.

A major deterrent to effective negotiating is the tendency to view the partner's behavior in all-or-nothing terms. Expecting someone who is reserved to be the life of the party, for example, is unrealistic.

Demands for sweeping changes practically always overwhelm the recipient and result in a refusal. Consider another strategy. Begin with less than what is ideally desired but with a suggestion or plan that is more likely to be acceptable to your partner. Later, if the degree or change proves to be insufficient, further negotiations can occur. The change or preference request can be formulated in two ways:

1. What do I ideally want?
2. What am I willing to accept for the present?

For example, consider the husband who, as far as his wife is concerned, spends an insufficient amount of time playing with their two-year-old son. The wife ideally wants him to spend some time each morning before work and each evening after work with his son. The husband agrees that he should spend more time with their son but complains that mornings are too rushed for quality interaction. The wife is willing to accept her husband's offer to spend at least a half hour playing with their child each evening.

This couple's agreement, based on a more reasonable request, may work out quite satisfactorily; if not, at some future time it may be renegotiated. However, since movement in a positive direction has already occurred, additional requests are less likely to be overwhelming.

Here are some additional suggestions for negotiating and compromising to resolve moderately abrasive differences before they become severe:

1. At this juncture, the communication skills discussed earlier had better be adequate and operative. Without this, bargaining is very likely to break down and become ineffective rather than improve the relationship. If after a reasonable period of attempting to improve communication skills there is no progress, professional help should be considered.
2. Choose a time and make a formal appointment with each other for the compromise-exchange discussion. Pick an hour when interruptions are

unlikely. An ideal time is when both partners will be unhurried and relaxed. If there are several postponements of meetings, this may be an indication that one or both partners are avoiding a confrontation. Discuss this issue.
3. Each spouse should state very specifically what he or she would like or desire. For example, "I would like greater closeness" is too vague and general. More specific statements that would be instructive to a mate might be "I would like to eat dinner together," or "I would like to spend time each evening discussing the day's events."
4. Begin with what is wanted rather than what is not wanted. Since both partners may have the tendency to use the exchange session as a forum for condemning the other, it is wise to focus on increasing desired behavior until confidence in the procedure and in each other is established. For example, "I would like more statements of appreciation" is positive, whereas "I want you to stop picking on me as you have been" may lead to an argument. Avoid evaluative, right-and-wrong types of statements. Consider differences as just what they are: differences.
5. Avoid using outside standards to express what is wanted. There is less likelihood of resistance when other people's standards are not used to measure against. For instance, rather than saying "Why can't you be like Ed Jones?" simply state what you want without the comparative reference.
6. When the change requested is outside the behavioral repertoire of a partner, steps to improve or gain the behavior should include a plan for mutual involvement. For example, if both decide that the wife needs more schooling to increase her earning power, perhaps the husband will take on additional household responsibilities to make this feasible.
7. Do not try to negotiate feelings. Feelings are not changed by bargaining. "Okay, I agree to be happy about vacationing with your parents" just won't work. Only behaviors can be negotiated; and only those behaviors that do not compromise a person's integrity are open to negotiation.
8. One of the difficulties that may occur in negotiating differences involves communicating the importance of a particular preference or issue. In this regard, particularly for the less complex issues, using a zero-to-ten rating scale to indicate the relative strength of a preference can prove useful. (Zero represents total disinterest or displeasure; ten signifies total enjoyment, enthusiasm, agreement.) For example, a man may want his partner to attend a work-related function with him. His partner may opt for a

party given on the same evening in honor of their next-door neighbors who are moving away. Using the rating scale (he gives his function a six, she gives the neighbors' party a nine), each is provided with an immediate and clear-cut idea of the strength of the partner's feelings. In this manner, many confusing, nondirective statements are eliminated: "I want to if you want to... but do you really mind... Well, maybe we shouldn't... I don't care, it's up to you."

The rating scale is particularly useful for couples who have difficulty expressing the intensity of their preferences. Use of a rating scale, however, should not put an arbitrary end to the matter being discussed. It is best used as one ingredient to consider in the overall discussion of differences. What's more, rating requires making an honest appraisal. Manipulative individuals who consider most of their preferences as tens will soon find their partners unreceptive to this suggestion.

9. Be patient. Compromise-and-exchange agreements are difficult. Do not expect to arrive at a mutual agreement immediately. Several discussion sessions may be necessary, even on seemingly minor issues. Severe and long-lasting differences may require professional assistance for successful resolution.

Tool Kit

Better negotiation skills can make you happier at home, more successful at the office, and more personally effective in any group situation. It doesn't come naturally to everyone, but anyone can learn to be a more effective negotiator. Here are additional suggestions that will prepare you for fine-tuning your discussions and strengthening your problem-solving skills:

1. Compose a list of the major criticisms you have about your partner. Now, sit down facing your spouse and reverse roles. Take turns speaking *as if you were your partner*, and express his or her feelings about one of the items on your list. Get into the role and present as thorough an understanding of this issue as possible *from your partner's point of view*. For example, a husband playing his wife might take an item from his list of complaints about her and say, "I'm really tired after a full day's work, cooking dinner, and putting the children to bed. I know you get annoyed if I fall asleep early, so I try my best to stay up. Sometimes, though, I'm so exhausted I just can't make it." Try to really get into the experience of being your partner

and understanding things from his or her viewpoint. Continue alternating until each of the criticism lists has been completed.

The ability to be compassionate toward a partner begins with attempting to understand him or her. Take a few minutes to discuss your experience with this exercise. What did you learn about your partner? About yourself? See if you can get into passionately defending your partner's (as well as your own) right to be fallible. Remind yourself of the acceptance equation when you are feeling intolerant of your partner: being human-being fallible.

2. Human beings are great "should-makers." We are sufficiently egotistical to believe that because we would prefer that something occur, it *should* occur. The behaviors we view as more desirable in our partner *should* replace those deemed less desirable. Seldom do we stop to think, "Whoever guaranteed us that the world [our world, our family members] was designed to conform to our demands?" In the acceptance experience below, we will increase our awareness of the absurdity of the "should" rule.

"Each partner is to alternate beginning a sentence with "You should _____" and complete the statement with the demand that your spouse be different. For example, "You should be neater!" It is very important that as you express your "should," you take the role of a parent scolding a child. Raise your voice, literally talk down to your partner by standing up and hovering over him or her, pointing your finger, and scowling. Do you feel somewhat like a nagging parent with your spouse? Now face each other, make good eye contact, and touch each other. Say the following sentence to each other, and pause to absorb what you experience as you do this: "I may not like some of your behaviors, but I value you overall."

3. Many of us are caught up in negativity, so much so that we are more alert to unpleasant occurrences than to pleasant ones. Some positive occurrences are taken for granted, some are minimized or even misunderstood, and occasionally some are silently noted. It is likely that most of us would like to hear statements of appreciation more often, which is the objective of this experience.

Sit facing your partner, and take turns beginning a sentence with "I appreciate _____" and go on to state your appreciation in sufficient detail so that your partner has a good sense of what it is that you find pleasing. Take about five minutes to do this. If you get stuck, just begin the sentence "I appreciate _____," maintain good eye contact with your partner, and see what words come to you. Allow ample time to discuss how you felt as you gave and received appreciation. Be sure to include in your discussion the topic "How I can bring my appreciation of you into our daily living." Conclude the discussion when both of you have offered at least one viable suggestion for increasing expressions of appreciation.

4. Recognize "his" and "her" conflict styles. Men and women have different conflict styles as well as intimacy styles. Respect the differences. A man may, for example, feel emotionally flooded and need a time-out while a woman may view that as withdrawal. If the man reassures her that he is simply taking a few minutes to regroup, his partner is likely to abide.

Here is a review of guidelines for constructive discussion:

- **Stay focused.** No fair dredging up mistakes made twenty years ago or complaining about how much the in-laws are hated. A fight is not an opportunity to rehash old grievances. Stick to the issue at hand or the discussion will surely sink beneath the weight of the problems.
- **Define issues.** Be clear and specific about the problem. This will help you stay on track.
- **Listen.** Really, listen. Don't just pause until it's your turn to speak again, with your mind formulating the next sentences while your partner talks.
- **Don't interrupt.** You can be angry without being rude or bullying.
- **Don't personalize.** Stay with the issue rather than attacking the person. Contending that your partner betrayed you in some manner is legitimate; calling your partner names, belittling, or otherwise verbally assaulting is not constructive.

A caveat: The idea is to over-learn these skills so that they are accessible when they are most needed, during the heat of confrontation.

Discussion Forum

Begin a discussion that is more conciliatory in tone and focus on an issue that has not been resolved. Continue your discussion until you agree that you have moved forward on this issue, even if you have validated each other's position but have not reached resolution.

> Self-righteous anger is the great thief of love.

STRATEGY SEVEN

Grow Your Children Effectively

Team Building

Do you play well with others? If you're a part of the working world, playing well with others means being an effective member of a team. It's a key part of nearly every job description. As business has changed over the years, with tasks becoming so complex that no one person has all the skills needed to accomplish them, so have the factors needed to excel.

In the less complex environment of years past, team-building and teamwork were not as critical as they are in the current business environment. New challenges demand new talents. Indeed, in a study by the Center for Creative Leadership reported by Lyle Spencer and Signe Spencer in their book *Competence in Work, Models for Superior Performance* among top American and European executives whose careers derailed, the *inability* to build a team was one of the most common reasons for failure.

Teams seem to be everywhere in business these days. There are management teams, task forces, quality circles, learning groups, and self-managed work teams. And that's not all; there are also the instant, ad hoc teams called into action as a result of a newly discovered need, and the short-lived virtual group working together on a one-time project. About half of Fortune 1000 companies report that they are using self-managed work teams and expect to expand their use in the coming years. The rationale is straightforward; a well-run team offers more enjoyment and fulfillment, resulting in a substantial boost in productivity as well as reduced turnover.

While teamwork is essential in the workplace, nowhere is it more important than at home. Home is ideally a sanctuary, and if the home team is neglected, productivity, health, and well-being are likely to suffer. The need for family teamwork makes its most challenging appearance when children are part of the household. Parents are the team leaders and it is essential that they work together in that capacity.

Today's parents share the responsibility for being all things to their children, despite help from nannies in some households. There are many more single-parent families than in past years, double-income households are common, and the workday has expanded substantially.

In the past when three generations of family members lived in the same house or nearby, it was easier to raise children. The team was expanded, with a more generous division of responsibilities. Grandmothers and aunts could counsel and help a mother who was distressed; a couple that needed time to themselves to work out their differences could ask another adult they trusted to take over for a while.

Fathers and mothers could discuss their parenting problems with older and frequently wiser members of their family. And the children could find a loving adult with time to listen and to counsel—a sort of court of appeals.

Childless couples can sometimes reconcile their relationship differences and disappointments by ignoring the discords, pretending they do not exist. They can seek compensating gratification elsewhere, usually in their career; it is simple for both of them to have jobs. However, when there is a child, this shift of emphasis is complicated, and the child becomes living evidence of the impaired teamwork.

At home, just as at the office, being a team player is about managing emotions and translating them into effective communication. Given the strains and stresses in the exec household, that can be a difficult task.

Here is a young mother's experience. Rachel is the wife of a media executive who spoke with me about her distress:

> We had been arguing for months. He was consistently coming home later than usual. I was sure he was fooling around with his assistant. I constantly accused him, but he passed it off as a joke. When he did this, I pestered him about it even more, but he just ignored me or made more jokes. It nearly drove me nuts. I nagged him all the time but he didn't admit a thing. The more I bore down, the worse things got between us. All this wasn't doing Patrick anything but harm. He was nearly eight, and he sensed the strain. He started bed-wetting

again and even stammering. His teacher said he was nervous in school. Maybe that woke me up, woke both of us up. Not only was our marriage troubled, but we were creating a toxic home life for our son.

Games Nobody Wins

While some couples, like Rachel and her husband, get caught in repetitive fights and others may even stop talking, instigating a long-term cold war, other couples draw their children into their conflict and form a triangle, a harmful form of parental disharmony that is often overlooked and may well have the most deteriorative effect on the family team.

Triangulation weaves its way into all kinds of families—single parent, double income, stay-at-home dads, as well as the more traditional, stay-at-home moms. In each instance it has a disastrous outcome. While all of these family models present challenges to execs and their spouses, they are put at significantly higher risk when children are drawn into their parents' issues.

Parents create this triangle because they are attempting to avoid conflict, reduce intimacy, seek revenge, or deflect painful emotions in their own relationship by focusing on their children. Whatever the basis, the children are drawn into adult issues and become key participants in an indirect and destructive communication game.

For example, the wife may make one child her ally and the husband may choose the other; sometimes they bid for the same offspring and he or she may end up feeling like God's special gift to the world. A father deeply in debt who finances a new car for his teenage son, saying, "I owe it to him," is probably involved in this manipulative game of "You're the favorite," as is the mother who wears her threadbare coat for yet another winter so that her daughter can buy that new dress she simply must have.

On the other hand, in the game of "It's all your fault," a child's life may be made extremely miserable because his parents are competing to find fault with him (the "fault" allegedly "inherited" from the other spouse). This strategy is a favorite way of getting at the partner who is more sensitive to the child's needs, which is one reason why it is dangerous in a distressed relationship for a child to be a favorite of one parent.

This invites misuse of the child as a weapon. In extreme situations, it may even result in physical cruelties. In any case, the child is apt to suffer emotionally, either through overindulgence of his whims or severe deprivation.

Moreover, the parents' conflicts, rather than diminishing, are likely to be increased and their teamwork, rather than being strengthened, is shattered.

Here are some other variations of destructive games that inappropriately draw children into marital conflicts.

At six o'clock on Sunday morning, four-year-old Ronald Franklin burst into his parents' bedroom. "I'm hungry," he declared loudly, waking his parents, Jim and Fran. Fran elbowed Jim.

"You take him down," Fran growled. "I was up three times last night with the baby."

"I get up with him *every* weekend," responded Jim angrily. "When do I get a chance to sleep?"

"You slept last night while I was feeding Laurie," Fran shot back.

"Well, it was your decision to nurse Laurie. It prevents me from *ever* feeding her—day or night."

"Fine, you win," screamed Fran, now wide awake. "Come on Ronald, Mommy will give you breakfast. Poor Daddy needs to sleep."

The argument, sarcasm and all, was clearly not lost on Ronald, who had been caught in a team-dividing game of "I'm the Better Parent." "It's okay, Mommy, I'm not really hungry," he said quietly and ran back to his room.

Then there is the increasingly more common game of "Bad Parent," played when a woman earns significantly more than her husband. Susan is a high-level executive for a women's-wear manufacturer. She travels a good deal, and her husband, Robert, resents her being more successful than he is. As a strategy against her, Robert begins to pamper their only child, whom he wishes to alienate from Susan in order to distract her from her career ambitions.

He: *(disgusted)* You're not doing your job. Jeremy is being neglected.
She: *(angry)* You're crazy!
He: *(self-righteous)* What do you mean "crazy"? You're never around to take care of him. You're always running off.
She: *(insistent)* Jeremy gets excellent care. Since when did you become father of the year?
He: *(accusing)* How many nights have you been gone doing who the hell knows what and the baby woke up and I had to take him into our bed!
She: *(counterattacking)* What the hell are you taking a five-year-old into our bed for? Jeremy is well aware of my job and shouldn't

ordinarily have any difficulty with it. Are you forgetting the times he has come to work with me and gone on trips with me? What about that? What about the time I spend with him explaining how I always come back? What are you trying to create?

He: *(angry)* I don't like it, goddamn it!

She: *(accusing)* That's it! It's you who has the problem. You resent me having an independent life. Your male ego's threatened!

Eventually, Robert's destructive strategy succeeded to the point where Jeremy started recoiling from his mother when she returned home from her business trips. Susan and Robert were divorced a year later.

Another common form of team-wrecking occurs when children are used to undermine a mate's authority and power. One partner may do this by subtly or overtly encouraging or assisting the children in breaking the rules established by the other partner. For example, as the father backs down the driveway, he notices the children's toys in his path. He gets out of the car, throws the bicycles, baseball bats, trucks, and skates out of the way, dashes into the house, and shouts, "Goddamn it, Gail! Have the kids keep the driveway clear. They have plenty of room to play all over the place. The driveway is off-limits!"

That night, returning from work, he hears the crunch of toys under the car wheels as he pulls into the driveway. He is furious. Storming into the house, he finds the family at the dinner table. Repeating the morning scene, he screams, "Who the hell left the toys in the driveway! How many times—"

Gail, looking relaxed and unhurried, replies coyly. "John, it's probably my fault. I was on the phone with Joan Edwards, you remember her, the one you found so attractive at the Smiths' party last week, and I completely forgot about talking to the children." The husband turns, slams the door behind him, and closes the first act of "I'll Get You."

A related ploy for expressing hostility and creating an obstacle to teamwork is "Victim/Villain." In one typical case, Nancy returns from shopping late on a Saturday afternoon. Her children had been assigned to do the dishes in her absence. As she drives up to her home, she honks her horn, but nobody comes to help with the shopping bags.

The kitchen is a mess, nothing's been touched, and dishes are everywhere. Furious, she races upstairs, shuts off the blaring television, and angrily confronts her two children, ages ten and twelve. She yells, "What is the meaning of all this? How could you be so inconsiderate?"

At this moment, her husband, Henry, who was reading his newspaper in the backyard, appears and is requested by Nancy to intercede. In complying with his wife's request, Henrys' tone and manner allows his children to see that he is condescending to their mother. He implies, *My heart really isn't in this, but I'd better say these things to get your mother off our backs.* In admonishing the children, he manages to create an image of himself as fellow victim and of his wife as villain. He is widening the gap between himself and his wife, and between his wife and the children, to the eventual disadvantage of all.

In all these manipulative games, the issue is not parental disagreement about the children's behavior. It is about using the children as pawns in the war between their parents. In each instance, the parents are divided and the leadership in the family is diminished.

On more trivial issues, parental agreement is not critical. Nevertheless, the behavior depicted above is the result of hidden agendas, and to focus on parenting techniques would be to miss the point. The critical issue in each case is underlying hostility communicated to a mate through the children, to everyone's detriment.

Jim and Martha's fight about their children that turns out not to be about their children at all may provide additional clarification:

She: You're too soft on the kids. You can't just let them do whatever they want.

He: I don't know what you're talking about. I simply told Bobby I'd rather he didn't go over to his friend's house, I didn't insist, and he decided to go anyway. Is that a crime?

She: That's not the point. It's because you don't insist that I have to take all the responsibility for the kids. Who disciplines them? Me!

He: I don't agree. I do my part. What the hell is bugging you?

She: *(angry)* You're driving me crazy! I do all the dirty work. You prance through life without a care in the world. What is this? If you're not going to be home half the time, the least you can do is face up to your responsibilities when you're here—

He: *(interrupting)* You're angry because the kids and I have such a good relationship. You're always trying to make me the heavy.

She: Oh, bull!

He: Listen. I take enough responsibility trying to earn a living. I think I deal with the kids just fine.

She: How do you know how well you deal with them? You're away so much of the time, you hardly see them—

He: *(uncomfortable, interrupting again)* Come on, let's forget this, we're not getting anywhere.

Jim and Martha thought they were battling about parental authority, doing a good job of raising the kids, and the role of the man of the house, but these proved to be superficial issues camouflaging more intimate ones that neither dared confront.

It emerged that Martha felt left out of Jim's life; unattended, unattractive, and jealous of the time he devoted to his work. When Jim and Martha sought marital therapy, Martha learned to level with Jim about her real feelings, wants, and expectations. The issue of disciplining the children was never raised again.

Yet another tactic used to wreak psychological havoc is employed by the parent who makes abusive remarks about the other parent in the presence of the children.

This usually produces embarrassment and anger in the offended parent and is quite unsettling to the children. Often the accusation is delivered in the heat of battle with the children present: "Don't give me that 'control yourself' crap. Why don't you control your boss and try holding a job for a change!" The rationalization here is "It's better to be honest with the children." But, of course, this type of fraudulent honesty is likely to put the children in the center of a game of "Charge and Countercharge."

Also under the guise of being "honest with the children," one parent may be covertly pleading, in a game of "Poor Little Me." Margaret, a fourteen year old, described her experience with this parental maneuver to me.

> My parents seem to be always fighting. They fight over the most ridiculous things. Sometimes, when they're both home, I go to a friend's house just to get some peace and quiet.
>
> Last Saturday my father suggested we take a ride to the beach. Just him and me. When we got there, we walked around a little, then we sat and talked. He told me my mother was a sloppy housekeeper, a selfish person, and a bad wife. He said he tries very hard to be a good husband and a good father but that my mother makes things hard. I was so embarrassed and uncomfortable; I didn't know what to say, so I just sat there frozen. I didn't say anything to my mother, but a couple of days later, she started to talk to me, and she said the same things about him! She said she tries to make us a decent home, but my father is immature and doesn't want the responsibility of a family. It was disgusting. I felt so alone.

The parental games described above and their endless variations allow marriage partners to show superiority, cover up guilt feelings, hurt a mate, avoid intimacy, and feel justified in giving up. These results are shortsighted, and the tactics are relationship-defeating because they conceal the real issues and sabotage family teamwork.

Children's Games

Children also develop defensive games as a refuge from their own emotional distress stemming from a lack of united parent leadership.

Joanne and Lew Koch have described a rather dramatic example in their book *The Marriage Savers*. Psychiatrist Paul Soloman treated Ruth, a seven year old with symptoms of serious asthma. Dr. Soloman suspected that Ruth's asthma was related to family problems and decided to approach her condition using family therapy.

During therapy discussions, every time Dr. Soloman got close to some of the real problems in the family, the child would get sick and threaten to die. After he had worked with the family for nearly a year, focusing on the parents' relationship, Ruth said, "I think that I should be sick for the rest of my life."

The mother said, "Why in the world would you say something like that?" The seven year old child answered, "I've figured out that when I'm sick, the two of you know what to do, and when I'm not, the two of you don't know what to do. If I'm sick, you don't fight. If I'm not sick, you fight." When Ruth's parents' relationship improved, so did her asthma. Dr. Soloman reports that Ruth had not been hospitalized or even seriously ill for three years following family therapy.

"Buffering" is another tactic a child may use to bring the team together. It is not unusual for a child to drift into the role of mediator during arguments. Most often, he becomes a buffer because he cannot tolerate the conflict ("If they split, where does that leave me?") and because his parents, perhaps sharing a similar fear of their own, become dependent on the child mediator to maintain an illusion of tranquility between them. The following conversation involving a child and his parents in my office illustrates the process:

Husband: Damn it, Jane, I get so angry when you spend enormous sums of money on such ridiculous crap.

Wife: That's just like you. When I spend money, it's ridiculous. When you buy something, it's a necessity. You see things in such a one-sided way.

Child: I got into a fight in school today, and I had to sit in the principal's office.

Wife: Paul, you shouldn't be fighting. Someone could get hurt.

Husband: If there's a problem in school, you tell the teacher. Don't use your hands on anybody. The teacher will help you talk it out. Okay?

Masquerading as a "naughty child," this youngster produces well-timed interventions to set himself up as a target and to divert his mother and father from further argument. He has learned that if he can turn their attention toward him, they will automatically issue a truce with each other.

Parents who are fearful of their deteriorating relationship, who prefer an illusion over real intimacy, are likely to be willing collaborators and reinforcers of the child's efforts. However, temporary armistices achieved this way are likely to have a damaging effect on the youngster. Once he is accepted in the role of peacemaker, he may feel at fault every time there is an emotional eruption he has failed to prevent. Continued distress between parents will result in escalated anxiety and disappointment in the child.

Instead of being supported and nurtured by his parents, the child peacemaker has prematurely assumed an adult role. In effect, the child relinquishes his childhood to keep the peace and bring the team together. The effort is futile.

When children consistently play destructive emotional games, it is often because their basic trust in their parents' ability to love and care for them has been undermined, and they believe they can get the love and care they want only through manipulation. Such children opt for attention even if it is negative. This yearning for attention that finds its expression in "impossible" behavior will diminish when parents provide a firmer foundation of love and security for the children. Children want the team to work! They want the leadership restored.

Other Considerations

Behind many children's games is the unspoken plea, "I want you to know how I feel so that you will stop doing things that are making me so anxious and afraid. Show me that I am all right and that you love me." It is not always easy for parents to view matters in this light. It is much easier for them to accept obnoxious behavior as revenge for punishments, perceived injustices, or other unrelated developments.

Usually these proclamations ("Jimmy's always been a nervous kid; it has nothing to do with us") are an avoidance of more serious issues. Sometimes, however, a child's emotional reactions are not directly related to or are out of proportion with marital conflicts. With or without parental dissension, the process of growing up is stormy. Peer relations, school pressures, achievement aspirations, dating problems, all take a toll on children; and parents often become the toll collectors because they're convenient.

Some children, as well as some adults, have inborn tendencies toward emotional distress and acting-out behaviors. This does not mean they are born with specific emotional and behavioral disturbances such as anxiety or violence, but they do seem to inherit tendencies toward irritability, introversion, or low frustration tolerance.

Recent studies at the National Institutes of Health show, for example, that from birth onward, children exhibit clear-cut temperamental differences. Long-term studies have demonstrated that the child who is inhibited in infancy and in childhood continues to act in a similar fashion into adulthood, while the energetic, assertive child is more likely to become an energetic and assertive adult.

Thus, an inhibited youngster who is naturally very sensitive may feel that his mildly angry parents are very angry at each other. Because of his overreaction, he may anxiously anticipate signs of another argument breaking out and again interpret the next mild conflict as a great hostile outburst, thereby creating more anxiety, feelings of insecurity, and so on.

This is not to dilute parental responsibility. The quality of the marital relationship and the manner in which conflicts are resolved certainly have an impact on children; however, they are not the only considerations. Children have their own problems, and their distress is not necessarily an indication that the marital relationship is faltering. Rather, their distress is both a signal to examine the situation carefully for the contributing factors and an opportunity for parents to work as a team in providing for their youngsters.

To Fight or Not to Fight

Children, whether they are naturally inclined to be sensitive or not, frequently become upset by parental anger and fighting, often believing themselves to be the cause of the conflict. This is particularly true of the chronically angry family. Given these realities, would it be best to spare the children this emotional burden by not allowing them to witness or be involved in marital discord? Many parents respond affirmatively, and with some justification.

First, there are times when the issues being discussed or argued about are too sensitive and therefore inappropriate for young witnesses. Second, and more important, parents who tear each other apart in front of their children in scenes reminiscent of *Who's Afraid of Virginia Woolf?* are creating a very poor marital model for their offspring. These are tactics to be aware of, and guarded against.

Specifically, when couples are mutually hostile, hurling contempt at each other, attacking each other's beliefs, feelings, and character, their children grow up displaying antisocial behavior. And when partners are locked in a pattern in which the husband withdraws in anger, the kids are apt to develop internalizing problems such as anxiety and social withdrawal. Children respond with increased distress, shame, and self-blame.

While intuitively it makes sense that ineffective fighting is harmful to children, social scientists in recent years have confirmed that chronic turmoil between parents does have serious consequences. For example, Dr. Martin Seligman and his colleagues at the University of Pennsylvania followed the lives of four hundred children for five years.

Some of the children were in homes where fighting was common, some in homes where the parents were separated or divorced, and the remainder in households that were reasonably harmonious. The researchers found that the children in fighting families fared just as badly as the children of divorce. Both groups were more depressed than children from intact families whose parents didn't fight.

The researchers hoped that the negative effects on the children would diminish over time, but after three years they hadn't. These children were still more depressed than the rest of the children, confirming the theory that parental fighting may hurt children in a lasting way.

In another report published in the journal *Developmental Psychology* (vol. 29, no. 6), psychologists John Gottman and Lynn Fainsilber Katz looked at fifty-six families over three years. They first evaluated the children between ages four and five, when the ability to regulate emotion develops. Three years later, the children of withdrawing men appeared to be mimicking their father's withdrawal. The children of mutually hostile parents had developed externalizing behaviors. Antisocial behavior was displayed by an inability to wait their turn, a tendency to disobey or break rules, and an expectation that others should conform to their wishes.

These types of patterns require professional intervention involving not just the child, but also the rest of the family. The primary goal of treating the entire family is modification of these debilitating family battles. Without intervention, far too many children are likely to grow up with emotional damage and to believe that marriage is an excessively troublesome and painful arrangement.

Considering the disadvantages, parents can decide not to argue in front of the children. The fact is, however, that simply not arguing in front of the children is a poor solution. Not only is it a virtual impossibility to have fights that the children won't become aware of, but a lack of open discussion actually robs the children of potential benefit.

The one critical guideline is to keep the fighting above board. Parental fighting in which both partners stick to the issues and do not resort to the crude, manipulative strategies exemplified by indirect and enormously destructive games actually helps prepare children for their own future marital fights and for survival in a very difficult world.

Marsha is a thirty-one-year-old woman who recently graduated from college and works part-time as a laboratory technologist. Marsha has been married for six years; she and her husband, Richard, an IT consultant who also works on a part-time basis, share the rearing of their two children.

Marsha described her parents' marriage to me:

They fought a lot of the time. You could hear them four blocks away, but I think they were basically happy. I remember many of their fights being followed by a resolution, a making up. They said things to each other in anger that they apologized for. They always made sure I was aware of the apologies. When they got mad at me, I was told, "Being angry doesn't mean I don't love you." When they were mad at each other, I was reminded of the same thing: "We may disagree about some things and feel very angry, but that doesn't mean we hate each other." They taught me that a person may not like something about you but still like you. This is a lesson that's made a critical difference in my life. Rejection, for instance, isn't as traumatic to me as it is to many people. I know, on an emotional level, that I can't be liked by everyone. Rejection doesn't make me feel worthless. I also think I am probably more assertive than most women. Being wrong or possibly incurring somebody's wrath doesn't frighten me. I've seen wrath, and it's not so terrible.

Richard comments:

I like Martha's folks very much, and I agree with her view of their impact on her. I think she was very fortunate to grow up in a household where people didn't believe in facades. Her parents don't censor themselves and display only their best side. They are very real. My parents, on the other hand, were petty, bickering, and indirectly hostile to each other. The display of emotion was taboo. I picked up a lot of bad habits. First of all, I didn't speak up when something bothered me. I would sit and stew. When I did say something, it was aimed at provoking guilt in the other person; I tried to get my way by using emotional blackmail. The disparity between Marsha's style and mine made for quite a conflict. It's been only in the last year or so that I have learned, mostly through Marsha's example, to speak up and say what I want and what's bothering me. No camouflaging. No beating around the bush.

It may come down to this: To the extent that unexpressive or passive parents wean themselves from the notion that peace and quiet must reign, they will have moved to a starting position for conflict resolution. This is possible without causing undue harm to their children. In contrast, those partners who are chronically angry are probably obsessed with the wrong issues and would do better to consider their posture in light of its potential damage to their family team.

Most important, fair fighting—fighting in which both partners are honestly striving to resolve a conflict rather than to destroy an opponent—can comfortably take place in front of the children. Ideally, children will learn by example to fight for their needs and express their feelings constructively.

Naturally, some issues (such as delicate sexual matters) should be aired privately. Dirty, underhanded fighting is best done secretly or not at all. If this is the highest level of fighting a couple can attain, they should consider professional assistance.

A couple can tell whether they fight poorly by the results: One or both partners is constantly hurt, and conflicts are hardly ever resolved. Issues involving the children that are repeatedly fought over but resist resolution despite compromise should be reconsidered.

What if the children were not the issue? Would another issue surface? If so, discuss it and see where it leads. Even under the best of circumstances, manipulative emotional games will be played—but as side events, not center-stage attractions. As parents become more aware of and are able to express their own feelings and their children's real needs, games of manipulation will yield to healthy and open communication.

Tool Kit

1. **If you are in conflict, direct your energy toward resolution with that family member.** Avoid deflecting your focus to someone else within the family (particularly a child).
2. **Review the patterns of interaction with your children.** The power of awareness is often underestimated. Once we identify a pattern, we can change it. Merely identifying a pattern often involves a change of attitude—in order to see it, a parent has to be open to the likelihood that he or she is a contributor.
3. **Calm down before interacting.** When you are distressed, it is particularly tempting to draw children in as allies or pawns used to avenge and temporarily alleviate your feelings. A calm individual can be an effective antidote to family anxiety and can help ease the resistance to change. Bear in mind that creating a strong team requires that you settle differences while respecting your partner. That can only be done when there is a reasonable containment of anger.
4. **If you can't settle your emotions, control your behavior.** Behave in a team-promoting manner that you'll respect afterward, even if your emotions suggest otherwise. In other words, ask yourself, "If I felt better, how would I handle this?" Then do your best to approximate that behavior.
5. **Do not use a child (regardless of age) as a confidant.** For example, trying to protect children by telling them what is wrong with the other parent may signal good intentions but creates an alignment with the "good" parent and will likely alienate the "problem" parent. Children should not have to choose sides between their parents. They need to discover their own truths without your influence. The only exception to this is the instance where a parent is a danger to a child who is too young to realize this.

6. **Consider that we all inherit the unsolved problems of our past.** That is, whatever is occurring with us in our family can be traced to the struggles of our childhood family. For example, the parent who is overprotective would be wise to look at his or her own upbringing. What is it in that upbringing that bears on your behavior in your present family? If we do not take this into consideration, we are more likely to repeat past patterns or negatively rebel against them.
7. **Keep the lines of communication open in the family.** While allying yourself with one of the children or talking to them about issues that should remain between spouses is off-limits, appropriate discussion is not. In fact, just the opposite is true. Children are very perceptive, and you do them a disservice by denying that anything is wrong. A statement that validates the child's perception without taking sides is warranted. For example, "It's true, Dad and I are working out some differences and sometimes it is a little rough." This states what is going on without casting blame.
8. **Be persistent.** It is important to keep in mind that changing a damaged parenting team is rarely a one-time effort, but a process that takes time. The process is often characterized by a step in the right direction that may be set back when pressure mounts.

Discussion Forum

Review item number six in the tool kit above and take a few moments to reflect on the patterns of your upbringing. What influence do you see in your current family? Have you replicated (or overcorrected) the problems of your childhood family? What were the best and worst elements of your childhood experiences with your family? Discuss all these questions with your partner and plan a strategy for creating a stronger family team, taking your past patterns into consideration.

• Superb teams are the modern grail of family life.

PART III:

Long-Term Development Plan

STRATEGY EIGHT

Protect Your Investment

Essential Competencies

In the rush and pressure of work days, our minds are preoccupied by a stream of business thought—puzzling out the current task, combing over our mental list of things undone, planning next-step strategies. The subterranean of mood often flows by unnoticed.

It takes a mental pause to attend to the feelings below the surface of our business concerns, a time-out that may not come until feelings boil over. When our emotions are crowded out by the pressure of the daily grind, it comes at a steep price; we lose touch with an inner rudder of conviction that is crucial for success at work, and as essential as oxygen in our personal relationships.

While many of us are dragged along by the strong current and pace of modern executive life, some people in the executive suite get it right and set an admirable example for all of us to follow. In fact, in a study of sixty highly successful entrepreneurs connected with companies having revenues ranging from $2 million to $400 million described in Lyle Spencer's 1993 book, *Competence at Work: Models for Superior Performance*, nearly every one of these high performers took time to reflect on their feelings, rather than depend on the traditional decision-tree method, which relies exclusively on logic.

In a similar vein, Richard Abdoo, the CEO of Wisconsin Energy, a $2 billion-a-year utility company, assumedly a very busy man, manages to reserve eight hours a week for personal reflection. "You have to force yourself to spend some time away from the hustle and bustle of your job in order to get down to reality again," he is quoted as saying in Daniel Goleman's book *Working with Emotional Intelligence*. "If you don't spend enough time doing that," Abdoo explains, "you can lose hold of the reins and get into all kinds of trouble."

What kinds of trouble? Abdoo was speaking of trouble in a business context, but if you don't spend time reflecting and expressing feelings in a marital relationship you are also in for trouble. The trouble usually manifests in a drifting away from each other, a slow insidious process that in the exec's marital life is the kiss of death.

The resolution? After experimenting with couples and trying it in my own marriage (weekly for two years), I developed the "emotional conference" and have found it to be a powerful, time-effective tool that is completed in a mere fifteen minutes a week. The emotional conference has a return on investment that is unequaled.

The emotional conference is an opportunity for a couple to be open—fully and accurately—by each person's expressing how he or she is impacted by their partner's behavior. The conference consists of a fifteen-minute date for a meeting at the same time each week. The agenda is discussion of feelings and reflection on where the feelings have their roots. Consider it a "date night" of a different sort.

Each partner spends five minutes talking about how the other's actions have affected him or her emotionally. The actions may have occurred at any time during the course of the relationship, all the way back to the first date. There is no statute of limitation.

While the main focus of the conference is the emotional issues provoked by each other in the relationship, the conference need not be limited to relationship issues exclusively. Such issues should definitely be given priority, but also of great value is the sharing of emotional issues provoked by people and events outside of the relationship—work, extended family, friendships, and the like. For these issues, all the guidelines and suggestions below also apply.

Interruption is not permitted. While one partner is speaking the other is listening. Each partner will mirror (that is, reflect back in summary form) what the other has said when he or she is finished. The two or three minutes of mirroring each provides for the other (immediately after their five minutes of speaking) accounts for the full 15 minutes of the experience.

The speaker should begin by briefly describing the incident and then describing how he or she was emotionally impacted. Further, if the speaker can relate his or her feelings to his or her upbringing ("I feel unsupported, just the way I felt growing up. My parents never had anything positive to say to me."), this will enrich the experience for both the speaker and listener.

It must be noted that this is *not* a gripe session, far from it. It is an intimacy-builder. The speaker is talking about his or her own feelings; the listener is learning how his or her partner responds emotionally, and about his or her partner's vulnerability as well as the origin of the other person's sensitivities. It is an opportunity to share your inner life—the core of intimacy—with your partner.

During the emotional conference we are not only expressing what we are feeling and thinking, but discovering how we have come to be particularly sensitive about certain things. In order to do this, you would be wise to give thought to your five-minute agenda throughout the week. Planning ahead assures you that your feelings and perspective will be well communicated, and that time won't be wasted in misunderstandings. In addition, spending time reflecting on your feelings will heighten self-awareness, an invaluable component in business and personal life. What's more, being a team player is about managing emotions and translating them into effective communication: the emotional conference is an ideal tool for this purpose.

The emotional conference directs the focus back on you and away from your partner. This does not mean, however, that we view ourselves as the cause of the problems or that taking the focus off our partner implies that we withdraw or distance ourselves. Rather, it means that we become better able to share our own perspective, to state clearly our own views and feelings, and to reveal who we are underneath the protective armor.

It is an opportunity to begin the self-exploration that is necessary for a deep and nourishing connection with a love partner. Of course, the goal is not just to move toward connectedness, meaning *any* kind of connectedness. Rather, the challenge is to move toward a connectedness that preserves and appreciates the individuality of each partner, allowing for real intimacy.

Guidelines

The few simple rules of the emotional conference are:

1. **Use "I" statements.** You are talking about your feelings, not casting blame on the other person. Briefly describe what happened, and then express your feelings. Then discuss what you think you contributed to the

incident. The incident might have been minor, or some major blowup.

The incident or issue (it doesn't have to stem from a particular incident or behavior) can also be something positive that has moved you; it doesn't necessarily have to be negative. What is essential is that you spend time before the conference thinking about the feelings involved and whether or not the feelings are familiar—that is, feelings you experienced as a child.

2. **Absolutely no interruptions.** One person speaks; the other listens. No exceptions. Turn off your internal dialogue and actually hear what the other person is saying. Also pay attention to nonverbal messages like facial expressions and eye contact.
3. **After the speaker is done, the listener reflects what was said.** He summarizes the major points, without editing, analyzing, interpreting, or judging. When both partners have spoken and repeated in summary form what the other has said, the experience is completed. There is no further discussion of what was said.
4. **Each person should have a separate agenda.** The second partner doesn't get to rebut what the first person said. Otherwise the conference degenerates into one asking, "How could you see it that way?" and the other countering, "Why don't you see it the way I do?" And that is just what you want to avoid! All too often love partners insist that they must share the same point of view, and this is what leads them into fruitless argument. Being different people, it follows that we will sometimes have a different view of the same events. Insisting otherwise is a prescription for unhappiness. Real intimacy requires a profound respect for differences. Don't make the mistake of confusing closeness with sameness and behaving as if you and your partner should share a common brain.

Bottom-Line Value

What is the point of the emotional conference? It is to give each partner the opportunity to consider how their actions affect the other, learn to listen attentively, reveal themselves, as well as manage to accept the other person's feelings without becoming defensive or dismissive.

The experience provides much more than a weekly reminder that no two people, even the long and happily married, view incidents and actions in exactly the same way. It provides:

- **A trigger reminding you to tend to your inner life.** Preparing for the emotional conference appointment requires reflection throughout the week and is an excellent method for cultivating self-awareness, the foundation of emotional intelligence. Indeed, Edward McCracken, former CEO of Silicon Graphics, is one of several leaders quoted in a *Fortune* article, "Leaders Learn to Heed the Voice Within," in support of getting in touch with our deeper, quieter voice of feeling. Self-awareness is our guide in fine-tuning on-the-job and relationship performance of every kind. Lacking that ability, we are vulnerable to being side-tracked when dealing with sensitive matters.
- **A safe format for expression.** Expressing feelings with sensitivity has salutary effects. Consider one example: When sixty-three managers who participated in a study at Southern Methodist University were laid off, they were understandably distressed. Half were instructed to keep a journal monitoring their feelings and reflections on what they were going through. Those that had an avenue of expression found new jobs faster than those who didn't. Volumes of research support this type of finding and provide an invaluable tool for personal relationships: The more we monitor and have an outlet for appropriate expression of our emotions, the sooner we can recover and move forward.
- **An opportunity to take responsibility for your feelings, in contrast to the destructive blaming pattern that is so tempting to fall into.** It will also assist you in reflecting on how your feelings link to experiences with your family of origin—the family you grew up with.
- **Practice in active listening, a valued competence.** Listening well is one of the keys to workplace success. Recall, The U.S. Department of Labor estimates that of the total time we spend in communication, the majority involves listening. In personal relationships, listening skill is essential. After all, an intimate relationship involves the sharing of hearts. One signal that attentive listening—which takes time and practice—is occurring is when you hear only one voice, that of the speaker, instead of two voices, the speaker's and your inner voice responding. I call this "quiet" listening.
- **The experience of building emotional muscle by remaining calm in the face of feelings that may be provocative.** In the workplace, this competence is evidenced among superior managers and executives who balance their assertiveness and drive with self-control. At home

it is the ability to listen deeply, tuning in with accuracy to your partner, and creating an environment that is emotionally safe; an environment that promotes trust and openness.

Let's look at an example of a couple going through the conference experience:

Frank, thirty-nine, and June, thirty-four, had been in a relationship for eight years and found that they were fighting nearly every time they were together. Their fights were instigated by things that barely made sense to them. They involved June's complaints about the lack of time spent together and Frank's not calling when promised, working too late, reading at the kitchen table, and not answering her pages.

Frank's arguments involved his contempt for June's complaints about him. He took every opportunity to point out to June that she had become dependent and unable to take care of herself—he often became infuriated at her for minor infractions like driving the car low on gas and forgetting to buy something at the market.

June countered that she simply wanted to spend more time with him and that had nothing to do with an inability to take care of herself. "You act like you don't like me," she told him with tears in her eyes. "I can't remember the last time you had something nice to say to me. All I hear is you being defensive and never admitting to anything. It seems I am always wrong in your eyes."

"And you have made me too important in your life," Frank snapped. "I feel smothered by you. I never get any time for myself. I am either working or with you, getting blamed for the time I am not with you. I can't stand it anymore. Get a life!"

Like most of their adversarial exchanges, the words they threw back and forth at each other became increasingly harsh until they both felt demoralized and pessimistic about the prospects of ever recapturing the happiness they once shared. Here is a glimpse at their backgrounds. Frank's mother struggled with depression all during his childhood. Every problem his mother had somehow became his father's fault. His mother seemed to hate his father and, consequently, she often confided in Frank and turned to him for comfort. The pressure he felt from his mother to fill in for his father had caused him to be resentful and influenced him to keep busy as a way to escape from her. He felt the responsibility for his mother's feelings had fallen from his father to him.

June recalled her parents' being so disorganized and so heavily embroiled in conflict with each other that they had little time or energy to pay attention to her. She rarely had any special time with her parents, especially her father, an aspiring inventor. Her father spent futile months huddled in the basement with each new project that he dreamed was going to bring him fame and fortune. June never felt important to him. While she acknowledged that her childhood household had had many positive elements, the pain of rejection is what she remembered and felt most sharply.

Frank and June began their first experience with the emotional conference hopefully, but it was not long before they had regressed to their familiar pattern. Each of them contended that the other was at fault for the conference not going well. Frank was convinced June had misunderstood the directions; June was absolutely certain she was correct and that he was wrong. Furthermore, she felt she had taken responsibility for the conference's occurring. She resented Frank for putting it off until the last minute, not giving it (and her) priority. "Typical of him," she blurted.

In the early weeks of the Emotional Conference, they continually interrupted each other, challenged each other's "inaccuracies," and began innocent discussion afterward that erupted into arguments. Both of them were discouraged and they wanted to discontinue the conference. Something, however, kept them at it. Perhaps it was the feeling that if they could only stick to the guidelines it would go better and help them heal the emotional pain both of them felt. And that is what happened several months later, in my office. Frank went first. Looking directly at June, he said the following:

> When you took a car trip out west a few years ago, the thought occurred to me that I wished you would have a fatal accident so I would be free. I wouldn't be a "shit" that abandoned you; I would be the poor guy who lost his love. A dark seed took root in my mind at that time. As irrational as it is, a profoundly disturbing idea haunts me: On the day that thought blinked to life in my head I had turned bad. I was tested and found wanting. My rational mind tells me lots of couples struggling with each other have such thoughts. The thoughts come out of desperation, not out of evil. But my heart says otherwise. Since that day, I have been troubled by a primitive suspicion that in some cosmic account book, in some dusty ledger of karmic debts and credits, your unhappiness is being charged to my account. I feel guilty and have often found myself barely able to look you in the eye. Every op-

portunity I have to avoid you, I take. It is not because I dislike you or that I don't love you. It is because of my own feelings that I don't live up to what you want me to be. I feel guilty because I know you are a good person despite the differences between us. And now I realize that I bring to our differences my own issues with my mother, and I have taken out my anger on you, instead of placing it where it belongs.

June sat quietly and listened. She had tears running down her face, and Frank looked as if he were straining to avoid becoming teary as well. She was apparently very moved by what Frank had said, but she neither offered comfort nor editorialized. She took in a deep breath and went on for about two minutes or so to summarize what Frank said in demonstration of her understanding.

In essence, she told Frank that she heard him say that inherent in the anger he had toward her was the demand he felt made on him as a child by his mother: "Take care of me; I am your responsibility. Your view of me leaves you feeling helpless, just like you felt with your mother. You have felt so helpless that you wished I would not be around anymore and that you were not responsible for that—and you felt like a bad person for having that wish. In fact, you have felt responsible and guilty that you were not making me happy and you avoided me because being around me made you feel bad."

Frank nodded in acknowledgment, and then June took her turn.

If I were to reduce all my feelings and their painful conflicts to a single name, I can think of no other word but "shame." It was shame, shame and insecurity that I felt in all those hours spent in pursuit of my father for the simplest recognition. Getting "Hello," when he came in the door would have been a start. I felt ashamed by my neediness, shamed by the hunger in my soul that I considered forbidden and weak. I thought I had gotten over that by the time I met you, and I believed you were different and it would be different between us. I am not happy about how I've acted with you. My hunger triggered the same pattern of chasing after you that I had done with my father. And the rejection I felt was the same experience I had with my father, making it all the more painful. I don't think it is fair for me to expect you to make up for the neglect of my father. I realize that the more I wanted from you and the more intense I became about it, the more it pushed you away. Rather than stepping back and seeing that, I became angry and more aggressive. That was a mistake for myself as well as for you, and I regret it.

As June had done, Frank sat quietly, kept his eyes on her and listened carefully. The images that had floated across his and June's minds—particularly the emotional wounds of their childhood that had been playing out in their marriage—were not comforting. Rather than thinking his own thoughts while June spoke, as he had done for the first few months of doing the conference, Frank did his best to focus on her words and the meaning they had for her. When her statement was completed, he mirrored back what she said, as she had done for him.

In essence, he told her, "You feel ashamed about feeling needy; feeling that helplessness you felt as a child chasing your father for attention. You don't like how that feels. Buried in your criticism of me is your wound from childhood. You have been saying to me in a variety of ways: 'Why can't you make me feel as if I count? The way you view me makes me feel invisible and I want to be seen.' You regret feeling so insignificant in relation to me and don't want to continue giving me responsibility for how you feel."

Although that particular conference was a turning point, Frank said, "it didn't occur until after we had been doing the conference for some time. It took us a while before we felt safe enough with each other to really be deeply open. In fact, while we were driving one day after we had only done the conference a few times, I was thinking about really being honest about my feelings. I turned to June and asked her to promise not to bring up anything I say in the conference and use it against me. She readily agreed and then asked me to promise the same. I did.

"Despite the promises we were both pretty frazzled some evenings after the conference. It wasn't easy hearing what the other person said and not reacting. I confess that there were some nights I was talking to June for a few hours about what she said—talking to her in my head, not directly to her. Now all that inner chatter has quieted down. And I am happy to say that we now look forward to Wednesday evening, the night we do the conference."

"The conferences didn't have an immediate impact on our relationship," June said, "but slowly it brought us closer. Our bickering eventually just decreased and then it stopped. Both of us became more relaxed, more open, and secure about our commitment. For a long time I experienced a sense of relief as a result of being able to talk openly without fear of fighting or reprisal, but I was also frightened and embarrassed. We both felt a little foolish that in all the years we've been together, the issues we've uncovered—about the unfinished business of our childhood—should have been obvious, but neither of us made the connection before.

"Now that we have been doing it for nearly eight months we find that we interact with each other differently at other times as well. Rather than interrupting, or preparing a rebuttal when the other person is speaking, we really listen and try to understand. It has helped us to recognize our differences as people without insisting that we feel and think the same about things. We both realize that we have different sensitivities and that it is important to respect that. Frank doesn't have to respond to the same things in the same way I do, and he gives me the same respect. Coming to terms with that has been very helpful. Initially, we both found ways to have a discussion of what was said so that we could have the opportunity to influence the other's viewpoint. We eventually stopped doing that. Now we hear each other and mirror, but we don't discuss what was said at all. It provides a good opportunity to accept the other's feelings without diluting them."

Accepting the other person's feelings, as June states, gives each partner the opportunity to get used to the notion that he or she does not and cannot control how other people think about you. Since many of us have not fully grown out of the childhood state of needing the approval of others in order to feel good about ourselves, taking in another's view of our behavior without seeking to "correct" it is a valuable experience.

Having a stable sense of "I" that is based primarily on self-validation rather than other-validation allows love partners to navigate the delicate balance between separateness and connectedness. In effect, if each partner has a solid sense of "I" it is easier to form the "we" in a relationship.

At the simplest level, having a solid sense of "I" means that we can be who we are in a relationship rather than what others wish, need, and expect us to be. It also means that we can allow others to do the same.

Developing a more solid sense of self as a result of doing the emotional conference regularly and in exact accordance with the guidelines outlined, will assist you to do the following with your partner:

- Present a balanced view of your strengths and vulnerabilities as well as what you've noticed yourself doing to avoid facing yourself.
- Make clear and honest statements that reflect your beliefs and experiences, past and present. This means that you are willing and able to reflect on how your upbringing has impacted your current relationship.

- Stay emotionally connected with your significant other, even (and especially) when things become emotionally intense.
- Address real (and perhaps painful) issues with your partner, not the pseudo-issues that sometimes are used to camouflage what really matters.

The emotional conference is a powerful tool that can contribute to the process of strengthening the "I" and repairing the sense of "we." It is deceptively straightforward, and if it is done conscientiously, it will prompt you to take time from a busy day to focus on your feelings, the emotional patterns in your marriage, and the patterns that you bring to your marriage from your family of origin.

The conference should occur once a week, but in circumstances where the issues have accumulated over time, doing it more often may be warranted. In addition, some couples find it especially helpful to keep a journal of the feelings expressed in the emotional conference for review.

Bear in mind that reaching the point where new habits—reflecting on and speaking about your feelings, listening deeply and non-defensively, avoiding blame and the like—are formed, takes extensive practice.

The emotional brain changes its habits over weeks and months, not days. "Overlearning," practicing a new approach far beyond the point when you can do it well, greatly reduces the likelihood that you won't revert to the old approach under stress.

Self-Soothing

The experience of being open and vulnerable, not only through what you say, but in what you hear your partner say, is not easy. Over time, doing the emotional conference will provide you with a more accurate picture of yourself and your love relationship.

If you bring in the links to your family of origin, you will also become increasingly aware of how your family gave you the blueprint for the relationship being played out with your partner. Your heightened awareness may be accompanied by strong emotions that need to be soothed.

Confronting yourself through your own reflection and expression as well as through the eyes of your love partner will almost certainly lead you to draw from your inner resources. No one is without vulnerability, anxieties, and problems.

The most important principle of growing, and this applies whether or not the relationship is supportive, is self-empowerment. Each of us is in charge of our own growth. Taking charge involves turning inward and accessing your own resources to steady your emotional balance. This is called self-soothing, your ability to be in control of your emotions, to comfort and care for yourself without excessive indulgence. It is the process of putting what is going on with you—the change and growth, which can be frightening—into perspective.

Indeed, managing our emotions is something of a full-time job. Much of what we do—from reading fiction or watching TV to the friends we choose—is in the service of making ourselves feel better. The ability to soothe ourselves is a fundamental life skill; most of us in the psychological professions view self-soothing as one of the most essential of psychic tools. It is difficult to envision being able to survive without the ability to withstand the emotional storms that are part of a deep love relationship.

Self-soothing is self-care but not self-indulgence. It does not involve emotional regression, or food or substance abuse. It does involve taking care of yourself while you're stretching the boundaries of openness and honesty with your partner. Self-soothing permits you to quiet and calm yourself. The process requires that you not give up on yourself, or tell yourself it is too hard to settle your emotions down. You have to stick with yourself, just as you would with a friend going through a difficult time. Here are some specific suggestions for soothing yourself.

- Do your best to stop the negative mental tapes. Stop "awfulizing" the situation and/or telling yourself, "How could he (or she) feel this way!" Accept the present reality; quiet yourself instead of exacerbating your very emotional state and losing perspective.
- To help regulate your emotions, review your past history and recall challenges that you faced successfully. Remind yourself that you are resilient. Once again, try to regain some perspective; reactions and situations don't last forever. Behave in a productive manner that you'll respect afterward, even if your emotions suggest otherwise. In other words, ask yourself, "If I felt better, how would I handle this?" Then, do your best to at least approximate that behavior. In contrast, when you start saying, "Maybe I shouldn't do that, but . . ." or "Maybe I shouldn't say that but . . ." take your own advice.
- If doing the emotional conference brings up a lot of family issues, as it

did for June and Frank, one of the most effective things you can do to release your emotional pain is to write about it. Set aside some time, and write letters to everyone in your family who you feel hurt you or let you down. No one needs to see these letters but you, so don't hold back, censor yourself, or worry about how well the letter is written. Just put all the hurt and rage that's been festering inside and contaminating your system on the page. You may also want to write a letter to yourself.
- An important aspect of self-soothing is to stop punishing yourself for past mistakes. Instead, write a letter of forgiveness. Look back at regrettable actions; recall who you were at the time. Remind yourself that you are a work in progress, ever evolving, always learning, and fallible.
- In addition to providing a safe and effective medium for expressing yourself by using the emotional conference, create a peaceful place inside you. If you can tap that source, you can stop distress from building up, allowing your mind to clear and focus more sharply. There are numerous ways to create calm: yoga, meditation, a walk in nature, a hot aromatic bath, a good massage, soothing music, prayer, deep breathing, pleasant memories, and so on.
- Lastly, keep in mind that the emotional conference is a growth and connective strategy. If you are finding it difficult, you are experiencing something positive, growing pains.

Discussion Forum

Discuss your availability with your partner and arrange a standing (weekly) appointment time for the emotional conference. Schedule a time when the children will not interrupt and there won't be other distractions. It is preferable that you find a time when your energy is at least at moderate levels.

Love will strengthen as I let myself be known.

STRATEGY NINE

Periodically Assess Progress

Measuring Performance

In *Working with Emotional Intelligence,* Daniel Goleman tells the story of the Donnelly Corporation, which supplies glass to the auto industry. A major customer kept rejecting large numbers of their products for being substandard, prompting three Donnelly production workers to drive four hundred miles to learn why the customer was unhappy with their product.

What they discovered lit a fire under them. Their customer was offering their employees a bonus for spotting less-than-perfect parts from Donnelly. Rising to the challenge, the Donnelly workers drove back to their production line and raised their quality control standards, being sure to ship only perfect parts.

The team at Donnelly had the right idea. Striving to improve is at the heart of great achievement. Whenever a team is open to feedback and finding ways to improve performance, they are on the path to accomplishing their goals. It is even a better idea to have a periodic feedback mechanism in place rather than waiting for problems to appear.

In a direct contact business, such as a restaurant, performance feedback comes daily. Not so in the exec marriage where days slip into weeks and weeks roll into months at rapid speed. If we don't schedule it, feedback may not occur at all, or if it does occur it may be delivered in a manner that is not helpful. Before we know it the old ways reassert themselves and we are in a familiar hole.

To monitor quality control and to cultivate new skills, periodic checkups are not optional, they are essential. As anyone who has ever lost weight on a diet only to gain it back can attest, the critical element is maintaining the desired change. And in most endeavors, especially in marriage, if you catch a problem early, resolving it is much easier.

The same applies to any successful business enterprise. Launching a product is only the beginning; monitoring and maintaining the quality of that product over time is the real challenge. Sustaining relationship satisfaction is a similar if not more complex process requiring fundamental rather than superficial change efforts.

New patterns of behaving must become part of one's lifestyle; temporary measures that are not periodically reviewed simply do not provide the ability to resist relapse. What's more, although many products manufactured today are subject to change as the marketplace evolves, nothing compares to the instability of a couple relationship where change is constant.

Just as adults go through life stages—the carefree twenties; the career-driven family-building thirties; the middle-age turmoil of the forties and fifties; the adjustment to retirement and mortality in later years—relationships also move through life cycles.

Partners in a long-term relationship can expect to begin their union spending most of their time engaging in pleasurable activities together without having to make many sacrifices. This is a time when there are few financial decisions to make, minimal household responsibilities, no child-rearing demands, and an undisturbed sense of freedom. Spontaneity is high, as is the novelty of sexual and companionship activity. The euphoria of this honeymoon period is suddenly replaced by responsibility and decreased freedom with the arrival of a child.

Roles will have to be renegotiated, and the desire for personal and career satisfactions often enters into conflict with the requirements of baby and child care. The "oneness" and romance that were characteristic of the courtship period have changed, and relations with in-laws remain to be worked out.

While both partners spend the next several years striving to prove themselves as capable, successful individuals, the line is crossed between "youth" and "middle age." Now parents of adolescents, roles once again shift as the woman in many traditional relationships returns to work. This is a period when a couple is struggling with many disconcerting issues.

Closing the gap created by their focus on the children is paramount. Add to this further role adjustments, midlife crisis, the stress of receiving job promotions that demand more time and effort, possibly losing a job, changes in family finances, and moving, and the load at times seems unbearable.

When the children leave home, there is the empty nest adjustment and then perhaps the most difficult transition of all: retirement. This requires a massive role shift by both partners. Occasionally, a couple that has stayed together to this stage despite important unresolved conflicts are forced to face their problems head on. No longer can they buffer their discontent with parenting or career concerns.

Even in this very brief and admittedly quite incomplete sketch, it is evident that relationships are constantly evolving. Each stage brings with it hurdles to overcome. Sociological studies have proven this to be true time and again. For example:

- Parents of young children show a marked drop in the amount of time they spend conversing with each other and a similar decline in social activities.
- Couple interests and couple activities fall off as a man or woman rises to more responsible job levels.
- Arguments over money tend to increase as a family's income increases.
- Sexual infidelity is more likely to occur when a man or woman reaches the middle years.

None of these findings warrants publishing the funeral notice of long-term relationships. What is indicated, however, is the need for *continued* application of the power strategies, supplemented with semi-annual relationship checkups. The checkup is a feedback tool.

Feedback lies at the heart of change and maintaining gains. Knowing how we are doing keeps us on track. If done properly, it is an early warning system to stem negative patterns—especially in the face of the stiff challenges of the exec marriage—and simultaneously serves as a confidence builder when we are doing well.

Preparation

Although sitting down and thoroughly reviewing your relationship may sound like a foreboding task, it is actually analogous to the kind of health-care checkup we routinely schedule for our bodies and even our automobiles—except, in this case, each partner is both patient and doctor.

It is also the kind of thing every exec does on the job. Quality control and performance feedback are, arguably, invaluable. In our personal lives, if done responsibly, with a format that encourages an honest exchange of information rather than the placing of blame, a relationship checkup can help both men and women learn more about each other's needs and desires. In so doing, it provides a sound basis for making constructive changes.

The questions in the relationship checkup that follow are intended to assist a couple in identifying and appraising the assets and liabilities of their relationship. The checkup is not intended as a test and therefore has no scoring mechanism; it is simply a means of developing information that can then be used to make a relationship work better.

The first step is to put aside an afternoon or evening when you and your partner can share several hours of uninterrupted time. Make sure both of you have the opportunity to read through the questions before proceeding together. That way you will be equally informed about the process in which you will be participating.

Begin the checkup by taking turns reading each question aloud, one at a time, allowing one to five minutes per question to record your responses on paper. Do not yet read your answers aloud. When you have gone through the entire checkup, allow enough time to reread the questions and answers to yourselves to see if you have anything to add to your notes. Do not rush your partner or allow yourself to be rushed.

The next step is to go over the checkup together. Take turns being the first to answer a question. (Your answers should be kept brief, with no comment given by the other partner until the first has voiced his or her complete response.) When both partners have had their chance to answer a question fully, the information that each has supplied should be discussed, pinpointing specific areas of satisfaction and dissatisfaction in the relationship. The final step, after identifying a problem, is to attempt to work out solutions by using the principles that apply.

You may not be able to discuss every question and answer in one sitting. In fact, you may have time only to deal completely with a few of the questions. If this happens, schedule another block of time within the next few days to continue the process, and make sure to keep this appointment. Follow this procedure until you have discussed all the questions and answers, and reinforced your relationship-strengthening abilities.

The Feedback Inventory

1. Is rejoining your partner at the close of the day a pleasant event? If not, discuss the most important reason for regarding your partner's return home as unpleasant. Be specific, for example: "Very often I return home to screaming children and immediate pressure from my wife to step in and settle disputes" or "As soon as my husband walks in he gives me the third degree: 'Did you pick up the clothes? Make those calls? Walk the dog?' I feel as if I have to stand inspection every evening." What are your *positive* suggestions for beginning the evening on a better footing?
2. Describe three aspects of your relationship that please you.
3. Is your sex life satisfactory to you? If you feel that it is not, what suggestions would you offer for improvement? Be specific.
4. Name at least two instances in the past two weeks when you have clearly expressed appreciation for your partner.
5. Name one thing your partner has done for you in the past week for which you felt appreciation but did not express it. What accounts for the lack of appreciative expression?
6. Recall two ways you have annoyed or frustrated your partner intentionally or unintentionally in the last couple of weeks. How could you have avoided doing the things that caused annoyance or frustration?
7. Recall two ways your partner has annoyed you during the last couple of weeks. How could these acts have been prevented?
8. Recall a quarrel that took place in the recent past. Did it culminate in bottled-up rage, hurt feelings, or resentment? If so, review the quarrel and discuss how it could have been handled more constructively so that it would have ended with an improved relationship instead of a bruised one. In the review, focus only on the negative elements that *you* brought to the quarrel.
9. Have there been occasions when you wanted to show affection to your partner and did not? What was the basis of the restraint? Give full details of the situation and your feelings.
10. Name two or three enjoyable activities you would like to share with your partner. If you are not sharing these experiences, what are you willing to do to make it happen?
11. What positive factors do you feel are missing from your relationship? Discuss each of the factors you feel is missing and what responsibility

you take for the void. For example, if you feel trust is lacking, discuss your difficulty in this area.
12. Describe one thing that you have requested your partner do, correct, or improve that he or she has neglected.
13. Describe one thing your partner has asked you to do, correct, or improve that you have neglected. What stopped you from being responsive?
14. For the unfulfilled request described in question 12, discuss the factors that, from your view, account for your partner's unwillingness or inability to please you. Bear in mind that reciprocity (you get what you give) plays a role here—be sure to include factors in your behavior that may discourage your partner's responsiveness.
15. Name one way in which you'd like to change. Would this change please your partner? What's stopping you from implementing the change? Don't point to anyone else.
16. Are you willing to listen and take your partner seriously when he or she wants to discuss personal and relationship issues? If this essential relationship skill is not as developed as you wish it to be, what is your plan for improvement?
17. If you have children, do they help or hinder your relationship? How so?
18. Under what conditions would you withhold important information from your partner? What suggestions do you have for creating more openness in sensitive areas?
19. What one factor would you like to see in place to facilitate more effective conflict resolution? What are you willing to do to make it happen?
20. What are your aspirations and expectations for your relationship in the future? Be specific. For example: "I would like household tasks to be shared equally" or "I would like my partner to become more affectionate." Name at least three aspirations. Describe what you are doing to ensure that these hopes will be realized.

Completing the checkup will serve as a reminder that a relationship, like any thriving enterprise, is always undergoing revision; change must occur if each partner is to remain responsive to the other's needs. It is this responsiveness that prevents or at least limits major crises and promotes intimacy.

Discussion Forum

Although the feedback inventory covers a broad range of relationship factors, there may be omissions that are pertinent to your relationship. Give this some thought and pose some questions to yourself that are likely to promote productive discussion.

> Forgiveness is love made visible.

STRATEGY TEN

■■■■■■■■■■

Maximize Resources

Making the Decision

When a company is floundering and the stakeholders are not able to effectively turn it around, it may be time to bring in a consultant to assess and address the problems. Strong coaching or mentoring helps employees perform better, enhances loyalty, and results in lower turnover rates as well as increases in job satisfaction.

In like manner, marital relationships sometimes require a consultant to help address serious issues that, if not attended, threaten to bring the company down.

Consider this statement from Howard Gardner, the influential Harvard theorist, from his book *Frames of Mind* (Basic Books, 1993), "My intelligence does not stop at my skin." To paraphrase Dr. Gardner's intention, it is an indication of wisdom to access resources when they are necessary and are likely to increase the likelihood of success.

A case in point: Barbara and Mark, who consulted with me have been married for twelve years and have two sons. During the last year, Barbara, the VP of a software company, had been involved with another man with whom she did business. She didn't know whether to leave her husband or to break up the affair and try to work on improving their marriage. She decided to work on her marriage and suggested to Mark that they go for couples therapy. Mark was bitter and complained that therapy would be a waste of money: "I'm not crazy. You'd better straighten yourself out or leave. I'm staying in this house; I'm not leaving my children just because you've had a change of heart. I raised them!"

Barbara wasn't about to give up her home or children. She continued her plea for third-party assistance until Mark reluctantly agreed to give therapy a try. Barbara and Mark give a summary account of their experience; Mark comments first:

> At the time Barbara suggested therapy, I was enraged. I'm a decent guy. I try to do the right thing. I've been home caring for the kids! This is what I get in return? I thought, "Goddamn it, I don't deserve this!" Besides being angry as hell, I was embarrassed. Going to a stranger and telling him that when I roll over toward my wife in bed I feel her tense up isn't my ideal way to spend an evening!

Barbara had this to say:

> I broke a cardinal rule by getting involved with a business colleague. It was the collision of opportunity and temptation. I knew I was driving Mark up the wall. He was starting to drink too much and he wasn't sleeping well at all. He was doing everything to contain himself. I really didn't see why I wasn't happy in my marriage. Why couldn't I get as much from Mark as I got from this other guy? Did I view Mark differently because he took on the house-husband role? I knew the only way I was going to work this out was with a couples therapist.
>
> One of the early things you said to us was, "I'm not going to make decisions for you; but I am going to help you clarify your issues and give you direction for healing the relationship. It will be up to you to follow through." I felt a little taken back by this statement. I guess I was expecting you to tell us what to do.

Mark:

> In therapy, I was encouraged to be more expressive and this felt good. I began to say a lot of things to Barbara that I hadn't said before. But things between us got worse. I said to you, "You suggested I communicate more, really express what I'm feeling, and when I do express what I'm feeling, what do I get back? Shit!" I was getting just what I got as a child. When I opened my mouth, I got a slap. You encouraged both of us not to give up, reminding us that pain is not a signal to run.

Barbara:

> "After five months of therapy, we began to see some real changes in our relationship. The biggest thing that happened was we began to ap-

preciate each other as individuals—adult individuals. I viewed Mark more as the man he is, rather than something less than the power-brokers I deal with everyday. I learned that he had been so preoccupied with taking care of me and the kids that he was suffocating. We did some reshuffling and it was a tremendous relief for him not to have all the responsibility of running the house. This was actually liberating for both of us. In therapy, we both began to appreciate—if not always like—each other's honest thoughts and feelings. We didn't feel we had to be overly careful about hurting each other or causing one of us to fall apart. We began to believe in each other's strength. I regret it took me so long to realize how much his support meant to me.

Mark:

Finally after several more months, we made a joint decision to terminate therapy. We wanted to do things on our own. It's not that all our problems went away. There wasn't anything magical like that. We just began to feel more like struggling with them without any extra help. I guess we had come to a point where we felt we understood and appreciated each other. We felt we could live our lives and be fulfilled even without each other. Also, for the first time in years, we were genuinely cooperative and positive with each other. We learned to compromise to our mutual benefit. Our relationship took a mature turn. We became more desirous of each other and truly enjoyed each other's company.

In this successful marital therapy experience, Mark and Barbara were helped in several ways, some of which may not be evident from their brief description. They learned how to

- Develop clear communication so that the message sent is the message received.
- Identify the behavioral patterns and attitudes that were causing their relationship to deteriorate.
- Take responsibility for their part of the marital disruption rather than blame the other.
- Practice techniques designed to increase cooperative, relationship-promoting patterns and decrease negative, relationship-eroding patterns.
- Develop the ability to negotiate and create workable compromises.

These are critical areas of intervention. To the extent that a breakdown occurs in one or more of these areas, relationship distress is likely to increase. A couple seeking assistance from a competent therapist can expect help in each of these areas.

Barbara and Mark got lucky. Without thorough checking, they ended up getting competent assistance. Don't depend on luck, not all credentialed therapists are the same.

In on-the-job coaching, an open, trusting relationship is the foundation of success. That was the conclusion offered by David Peterson in a presentation to the annual conference of the American Psychological Association. Peterson drew this conclusion from a study of fifty-eight top managers, all vice presidents or above, at companies with $5 billion or more in annual sales. Couples therapy is more complicated. Here are some preliminary screening suggestions:

- It is important in a prior telephone call or initial session to obtain information regarding the therapist's credentials and point of view.
- Beware of the therapist who imposes personal biases (e.g., insists on a particular lifestyle). This does not mean that therapists are not to have personal beliefs or that they are not to be expressed, only that they be honestly labeled as biases and not imposed.
- Therapists who view their role consistently as a judicial one, in which they sift the evidence presented and eventually make pronouncements are, at best, inexperienced. This approach tends to be extremely damaging because the spouses involved are likely to devote their energies to digging up evidence against each other. The result is an escalation of bad feelings and an increased schism until the therapy and the relationship break down altogether.
- Therapists who side with one or the other partner on an overall basis ("You're the problem") rather than as a temporary therapeutic maneuver or on a particular issue, are reinforcing the false idea that at the heart of couple problems is a victim or a villain.
- Accusing each other and blaming the relationship disturbance on each other is decidedly counterproductive. Bitter quarreling over pointless issues, particularly if it goes on session after session and is encouraged by the therapist, allowing the destructive behavior to continue, is an indication of an incompetent therapist.

Danger Signals

How does a couple know if therapy is warranted? Relationship distress may range from overt anger to underground dissatisfaction taking the form of avoidance. The most obvious "red flags" indicating that a couple should consider getting the assistance of a professional third party are these:

- Frequent arguments without resolution in which one or both partners are left with hurt feelings or burning resentment.
- Feelings of being mistrusted for real or imagined reasons, or being suspicious of your partner. ("How does she *really* spend her days off? She's always so evasive when I try pinning her down.")
- Frequent avoidance of each other. There are numerous ways people living together can avoid each other. Sometimes a couple manages to have other people around all the time—frequent houseguests, friends for dinner, friends to share vacations, friends to spend weekends with—hardly ever giving themselves an opportunity to be alone. These are usually the couples whose divorce shocks their friends who thought they were "wonderfully happy together." Television is another convenient barrier. Overwork or over-involvement in non-couple recreational pursuits can also be a danger signal.
- Over-dependence on the part of one or both partners. This can be expressed by constant "checking" on each other, not feeling comfortable and worthwhile without a mate's companionship, resentment of a mate's independent interests, living for a spouse's achievements, and being overly sensitive to a spouse's criticism.
- Sexual dissatisfaction. This includes lack of attraction, inability to "let go" in bed, a lack of affection, warmth, or mutual sexual pleasuring. Also significant are extramarital sexual relationships.

These are some of the more common danger signals; there are an infinite number of variations. When should you seek help?

Not after a short-lived, shallow dip in domestic satisfaction. A day's arguing over the children, a few days of melancholy or self-pity, a siege of jealousy; these are not necessarily signals of trouble. They are more probably results of the normal strain of living the exec lifestyle. The key is to watch for repetition, a continued feeling of resentment, boredom, loneliness, hurt, and sexual dissatisfaction.

What *Not* to Expect

When we are little children and we fall, bruising our knee, Mommy or Daddy kisses the injury and makes it all better. They do magic. When we go to the doctor and she gives us a prescription that cures our ailment, the doctor does magic. When we are grown up and have marital problems, we go to another type of doctor, the marriage doctor, expecting that he or she will make the marriage all better, like magic. Unfortunately, therapy doesn't work that way. There are no magic pills, no magic wands to wave.

A passive stance—"therapy will make us all better"—is an unrealistic attitude that guarantees therapeutic failure. This is probably the most common unrealistic expectation that couples bring to therapy, and it is probably similar to the erroneous attitude that the marital relationship will prosper by itself: "Now that we're married, the relationship will grow." Most of us are aware of the falsity of the latter notion, but it is a tempting trap. In actuality, a business works because the stakeholders work at it; marriage works because the marital partners work at it. This applies equally to therapy.

Other expectations that increase the likelihood of dissatisfaction with therapy are these:

- **Marital therapy is a process designed to keep the marriage together.** This is not true. Therapy is supposed to help couples clarify their own needs, wishes, and feelings and to identify in their spouses those traits that meet their needs and those that do not. The attitude of a professional is likely to be: My job is to help these people stay together more compatibly and productively or to help them separate as amiably as possible. Since this is not my marriage, it is not within my province to decide which of these two courses to take. Full disclosure: While this is the proper view, admittedly I am biased toward keeping the marriage together.
- **"The marital therapist, being an intelligent individual, will see my side of things and straighten out my spouse, who is really the problem."** Very often this is the hidden agenda. However, if the therapist takes sides, the therapy may seem to be going well for the "righteous mate" but the marriage is likely to deteriorate. A more productive attitude involves shared responsibility for the dissatisfaction.
- **"I should feel comfortable throughout therapy."** It is not comfortable to change old habits. Consequently, the therapeutic process is likely

to be painful at times. Serenity is hard to maintain while sensitive issues are being brought to awareness and confronted as never before. Also, the progress of the partners is likely to be uneven so that when one opens up, the other may rebuff him or her. Result: hurt and angry feelings. Sensitive therapists will support the rebuffed partner, encouraging that partner not to give up while helping the other to be more responsive. But it still hurts. Discomfort in therapy is unavoidable; and total absence of any discomfort is a sign that the process is merely superficial.

- **"If we are sincere and work hard, things will improve immediately."** Change is not easy and it is not instant. A relationship may even worsen before it gets better. Dissatisfaction, hurt feelings, anger, and misunderstanding are not quickly cleared up. Yet people tend, after a few sessions, to conclude things are all better. Frequently, this is a premature decision based on an avoidance of further exploration of "hot" issues.
- **"We can always go into therapy in the future; things aren't that bad now."** One of the biggest frustrations of marital therapists is that couples hesitate to seek help until the situation is desperate. Then they come to the therapist and expect to be bailed out of trouble. By this time, the relationship may have been severely damaged and the willingness of husband and wife to work at it almost exhausted. It is very difficult to help marriages that are extremely disturbed. They often break up in the end, and the partners unfairly ridicule the skills of the therapist when, in fact, King Solomon couldn't have prevented the breakup. If these same couples had begun therapy earlier, before things became intolerable and all caring stopped, they could have been spared years of marital suffering and misery.

Types of Marital Therapists

Successful therapy relationships depend less on the professional's title than on training, experience, and personal qualities. Yet knowing something about the classes of therapists makes for a more informed choice. The three major classes of mental health practitioners are psychiatrists, psychologists, and social workers. Professionally trained marital therapists, counselors, and nurse practitioners also offer treatment services to the public. A brief discussion of each follows.

PSYCHIATRISTS

Psychiatrists are physicians who have completed medical training and have obtained a medical degree (M.D.). Rather than formal training in the psychology of marital problems or supervised experience in helping persons solve their most pressing problems, many psychiatrists are primarily schooled in handling patients administratively with drugs and hospitalization, and giving psychological first aid.

Psychiatrists who have completed the requirements of the American Board of Psychiatry have usually spent approximately three or four years in psychiatric residence beyond the four years in medical school and a general (medical) internship. A part of the residency is usually done at a large mental institution such as a city or state hospital. In this setting, the people treated by the psychiatrist are likely to be severely disturbed, such as schizophrenics or chronic alcoholics.

Some of the training period, usually about six months, is spent working with neurological problems (disorders caused by pathological abnormalities of the brain or nerves) and some time is frequently devoted to work in an outpatient clinic, where the physician sees a variety of patients with a variety of problems.

Some psychiatrists doing psychotherapy and marital therapy rely heavily on medical methods, especially the administration of psychoactive drugs. This is most common among those with insufficient advanced training in individual and marital therapy. Such a psychiatrist is likely to prescribe drugs in an effort to "give the patient something." Unfortunately, problems of living are rarely solved by drugs.

How can you ascertain psychiatrists' methods of practice? Asking someone who has seen him or her in therapy may be helpful. A psychiatrist may briefly discuss his or her orientation in a telephone conversation.

If nothing is known except that a psychiatrist is qualified with an M.D. and certification from the American Board of Psychiatry, an initial consultation is wise. The couple should arrange to meet the therapist together and ask about methods and point of view.

Asking pointed questions of the therapist as to training, experience, and attitudes may seem rude or unnecessary, but remember that therapy is an important and expensive venture, the success of which depends, in part, upon the proper choice of therapist. Couples may have to visit two or three different psychiatrists before finding an individual with whom they both feel comfortable and confident.

PSYCHOLOGISTS

A professional psychologist is, with few exceptions, an individual who has a doctoral degree from an accredited university or professional school in a program that is approved by the American Psychological Association. The doctor's degree takes five years beyond the four-year college degree to complete. This includes a one-year supervised internship. All states have laws regulating the practice of psychologists. In the case of psychological practice that involves service for a fee (such as marital therapy), appropriate registration, certification, or licensing is required. All states forbid anyone not so registered, certified, or licensed to represent to the public that they are a psychologist.

Since a psychologist does not have a medical degree (in psychology the doctorate is the Ph.D., Ed.D., or Psy.D.), he or she is not permitted to prescribe drugs. If pharmaceutical therapy is deemed necessary, the psychologist will refer the patient to a medical doctor for consultation and a prescription.

All psychologists are concerned with the dynamics of personality and behavior but their training varies considerably. As a group, psychologists have far more extensive training in principles of human behavior than the general run of psychiatrist or social worker, but not all may have had specialized training in applying their knowledge to individual or marital disturbances. Some have a strong background in other areas, for example, treating substance abuse or anxiety disorders, that have only modest relevance to marital therapy, at best.

Psychologists in the private (or agency) practice of individual and marital therapy usually have a background in the more therapy-relevant specialties of clinical or counseling psychology, but it is wise to ask the practitioner about his or her specific experience. Psychologists who are board certified by the American Board of Professional Psychologists (ABPP) have passed a three-part exam demonstrating advanced competence.

SOCIAL WORKERS

The minimum standard for a professional social worker is a master's degree in social work (M.S.W.) earned by the completion of a rigorous two-year program of graduate study in an accredited school of social work. In addition to receiving the required classroom instruction, candidates for the degree work two or three days a week in an agency that offers counseling services, such as a psychiatric clinic, a hospital, a probation department, a welfare department, or a family counseling clinic.

This internship, spread over two years, is supervised by an experienced social worker who holds the M.S.W. degree. Usually, individuals accepted into a graduate school of social work have an undergraduate degree (B.S. or B.A.) in one of the social or behavioral sciences.

Most states have laws that license or certify the practice of social work, and there is national certification by the Academy of Social Work as well as strong local, state, and national (National Academy of Social Work) organizations that strive to enforce professional standards. Most social agencies are sensitive to professional standards and in only a few, such as departments of county welfare, is the term "social worker" used for individuals who do not have the M.S.W. degree.

A couple desiring marital therapy would normally not be applying for this service at a welfare agency, but at a family counseling service where the professional degree is required for employment. In seeking a private practitioner, an inquiry as to whether the individual has earned the master's degree in social work from an accredited institution is warranted.

It is important to ask the social worker questions regarding his or her professional experience. One pertinent question may be "Have you had supervised experience in marital therapy?" Typically, social work students are offered a general program during their two years of training. This includes group work, individual casework, and community organization. A few social work schools provide for specialization in one of these areas. Thus, a student interested in training in marital and family therapy may be assigned a family counseling agency for internship. Others may obtain specialized training after obtaining the graduate degree.

Although social workers are frequently given less status by the public and by other professionals, with appropriate training, they are as qualified to do marital therapy as psychiatrists and psychologists trained in this area.

MARITAL THERAPISTS

"Marital therapist" is a general term that can include social workers, psychologists, psychiatrists, pastoral counselors, and just about any individual who wants to use the term, credentialed or not. Unlike psychologists, psychiatrists, and professional social workers, the title "marital therapist" is not always restricted. However, to belong to the American Association of Marriage and Family Therapy, the practitioner must have a master's degree in marriage and family therapy or a related field, and two years postgraduate supervised clinical training.

In addition to the practitioners noted above, nurse practitioners have a master's degree or its equivalent in nursing with a specialization in psychiatric nursing and may also do marital therapy. Professional counselors and pastoral counselors are also licensed in most states and must have a minimum of a master's degree and post-graduate, supervised experience.

The Search

Finding a satisfactory therapist is often difficult. Sometimes recommendations made by friends, physicians, and lawyers are useful; other times they are not (a therapist who is quite helpful to one couple may not be helpful at all to another). Public reputation is often a clue, but sometimes the popular therapist is the one who pleases rather than effectively intervenes.

Some marital therapists without academic credentials are very talented. However, in a field where incompetence and fraud are not uncommon, it is safer to choose a therapist who has had reputable training and experience. Unfortunately, professional qualifications do not indicate whether a therapist has had minimal, uninspired, or top-quality preparation. Further, since all forms of therapy are a mixture of art and science, the personality of the therapist is also important.

A marital therapist may be a happily married man or woman who accepts life, marriage, and people, or a dour individual whose marriage is sterile and who approaches marital problems with a "what can you expect" attitude.

Sometimes marital therapists are very directive in their approach, to the point of becoming impatient or irritated if their clients fail to follow their suggestions immediately; sometimes they are so timidly non-directive that their clients feel they are providing the therapist with an interesting hour of conversation and gaining nothing in return.

Occasionally a practitioner will have a moralistic attitude toward sex, divorce, or life itself that is conveyed in judgmental proclamations about right and wrong. Or, the therapist may have an irresponsible, "liberated," egotistical attitude that causes confusion and uncertainty.

Even the best therapist with the best training is bound to have bad days, and is certain to do better with some couples than with others. However well intentioned, a therapist's interventions may not always be correct. The mark of a professional is not perfection; it is a willingness to admit mistakes and learn from them.

It should be clear by now that you must be cautious in choosing a marital therapist. Obviously, these warnings can be used to provide justification for those who wish to avoid therapy or who want to quit because the going is rough. This is not the spirit in which the cautions have been offered.

Competent professional intervention has improved many ailing marriages, and effective therapists have helped couples to reconsider their relationship and move in more constructive directions. This type of exploration is not being discouraged. The point is that to increase your chances of reaping the very real benefits of therapy, you should be able to evaluate a therapist with some sophistication.

In making a decision about a therapist, your own judgment is critical. A poor choice is bad enough when you're buying something that has only limited impact on our life. But you are depending on a marital therapist to help you repair serious issues. A poor choice can have far-reaching consequences. With an incompetent therapist a problem that may have been repairable can worsen to the point of no return.

Assessing the Therapist

Given the importance of the decision, after credentials, personal qualities, and reputation have been considered, the final decision as to compatibility rests on the couple's shoulders. The most effective way of deciding is to get referrals from several sources, including professional associations, friends, and other professionals, and to shop around.

Admittedly, this procedure can be expensive because a few visits to a therapist may be necessary before a reasonable judgment can be made. It is also possible that the first therapist chosen will prove to be quite suitable. To aid in making a realistic appraisal of the therapist, a list of seventeen questions follows.

Responses are scored from 0 to 4; 0 equals never or not at all; 1 equals slightly or occasionally; 2 equals sometimes or moderately; 3 equals a great deal or most of the time; and 4 equals markedly or all of the time.

Use a pencil to write in the number that best reflects your feelings and observations and then obtain a total score.

1. The therapist openly expresses interest in working with me.
2. The therapist uses words and language that make sense to me, not psychobabble.

3. The therapist listens carefully to what I say and asks relevant questions that demonstrate that he/she is paying attention.
4. In the presence of the therapist, I feel like a whole person, with some areas on which I need to work. I do not feel like I am ill, weird, or disturbed.
5. The therapist is open to different points of view. He/she is not fixed on one correct way of handling an issue.
6. The therapist gives me the opportunity to figure out solutions to my problems, rather than simply telling me what to do.
7. The therapist confronts me with his/her concerns when it is beneficial to my emotional well-being, even if I might not like what I hear.
8. The therapist does not resist giving me his/her direct opinions in emergency situations that require immediate action.
9. I believe that the therapist has my best interests at heart.
10. The therapist behaves in a manner that assumes we are equals; he/she does not place him- or herself upon a pedestal.
11. The therapist spontaneously volunteers aspects of his/her life when it is useful.
12. When I ask directly, the therapist discusses his/her personal life to the extent that it is beneficial to the therapy or to the therapeutic relationship.
13. The therapist is open to seeing other people in my life when necessary, or to giving me sound reasons for not inviting others into the treatment setting.
14. The therapist admits, nondefensively, when he/she doesn't know something.
15. The therapist is open to listening when I feel he/she has made a mistake. He/she reacts without defensiveness and is able to acknowledge mistakes when appropriate, or to explain his/her actions in a manner that makes sense.
16. I leave most sessions feeling hopeful and positive. Even when I leave feeling sad, it's not because I have given up hope that the therapy can help me.
17. Overall, I feel that I am learning a lot about myself and that I am improving the quality of my life.

A perfect score of 68 on this instrument is most unlikely. A rating above the mid-40s is an indication of a sound choice, a rating between 35 and 40 is borderline, and a score below that is indicative of a poor choice.

In marital therapy, it is important that the therapist chosen be acceptable to both partners, because a big difference in regard is likely to add to an already strained relationship. As mentioned earlier, it may take several sessions before a reasonable judgment can be made. Sometimes there is an obvious match and a much quicker decision will be rendered.

Cost and Length of Therapy

One of the most important considerations for many couples is the cost of therapy. The range is very broad, and is complicated by the number of managed care companies that set fees for therapists on their panel. If it is affordable, it may be advantageous to see a therapist who is not part of managed care, the advantages being increased confidentiality and continuity of care without the dictates of an anonymous case manager who would like nothing better than to have treatment terminated.

Community agencies and family institutes, both public and private, generally have lower fee schedules and may even have a sliding scale based on income. Listings of these agencies are available in the reference section of a public library or through a local mental health association.

Here are several suggestions regarding fees:

- It is wise not to become involved with a therapist whose fees you will not be able to afford on a weekly basis for at least several months.
- When there is legitimate financial reason, it is not "impolite" to ask if a therapist will reduce the fee in the initial phone call. Some will, others won't. Most won't offer unless asked.
- Do not regard size of fee as a reflection of ability. There is no relationship. Some competent therapists have a relatively low fee schedule; others bordering on incompetence are exorbitant.
- Whatever the fee, it is not unusual to feel resentful. Payment for an intangible service is hard to accept. Most of the money you spend affords you something that can be lived in, driven, eaten, worn, or shown off. Therapy provides none of these.

Just as fee schedules vary, so do recommendations concerning the frequency with which a couple needs to see the therapist and the length of time the therapy takes. In many instances, it will be suggested that therapy occur once a week, jointly, for forty-five to sixty minutes. Sometimes treatment is warranted more often, and sometimes less.

If the marital difficulties are quite serious, therapy is likely to continue for one or two years. It may be on a weekly basis, but more likely, as progress is made, the frequency will be decreased. Sometimes, although the problems appear severe at first glance, progress is established in a relatively short time and methods for continuing progress without therapy are suggested.

Regardless of the duration of therapy, it is doubtful that progress will proceed in a neat, forward direction. Rather, periods of stagnation, or even backsliding, are to be expected. Freud termed these reverses "negative therapeutic reactions" and ascribed them to an unconscious sense of guilt that barred improvement. While there is good reason to believe that Freud's explanation is ill-suited to the dynamics of many people, periods of "two steps back" and stagnation are part of even the most successful therapy experiences.

Discussion Forum

Review the "Danger Signals" section in this chapter with your partner. If either you or your partner identify with any of these points, discuss the possibility of seeing a couple's therapist, even if it is for a single-session consultation or perhaps a short-term tune-up.

Early intervention demonstrates wisdom.

PART IV

Best Practices

The Ten Power Strategies Action Plan

Hard Results, Soft Means

Although the directives in this book can bring about radical change—and, in that sense, they are revolutionary—the tool kits and bulleted suggestions that you have reviewed in the preceding pages are neither a formula for instant improvement nor a game or gimmick. They are, rather, a program of hard work and can be demanding and emotionally draining. Following this program can lead to occasional failures as well as to success, to brief periods of sadness as well as to exultation.

I do not promise a relationship devoid of problems. Not even therapy can elevate a relationship to a state of constant euphoria. Such a condition does not exist in life except, perhaps, in our fantasies.

Those who have decided to strengthen their relationship should be prepared to deal with all of this, for there is no such thing as growth without effort and setbacks. I urge you to make the effort. It is a wise investment; it is an opportunity to escape the chains of past disappointment and hurt by building constructively for now and the future.

Specifically, if the suggestions in the tool kits are studied and sincerely applied, several things are likely to occur:

1. Each partner will become more capable of contributing to the other's present and future goals.
2. Mutual support will be increased; both partners will enjoy a greater understanding of each other.
3. The degree of stimulation and companionship will be increased and expanded.

4. Disagreements and decisions will be collaboratively resolved.
5. Sensitive areas of the relationship will be explored more satisfactorily than previously.
6. The ability and willingness to adapt to changes that affect the relationship will be increased.

In the final analysis, each of us is the architect of our own relationships. Perhaps the best assistance a book such as this can provide is a blueprint for the creation.

Mutual growth is at times as painful and difficult as it is joyful and rewarding. Although it is not easy to develop, it is worth the effort. We are living in a period of rapid social change. Most people presently in the workforce were raised in families where Dad not only made most of the money but also made most of the important decisions. Currently, executives are often navigating unchartered waters: there are more stay at home dads than ever, the number of women who are higher earners than their spouse is growing, and we are experiencing the highest percentage of two-income households in history. At the same time corporate life is increasingly demanding and insecure.

Human relationships, especially long-term and intimate ones, offer something of value worth hanging on to. Even with its limitations, a committed relationship—whether or not it is sanctified by a marital decree—is, for many of us, one of the best and most enduring means of fulfillment.

In fact, our survival depends on the healing power of love, intimacy, and relationship. Although there is more scientific evidence now than ever demonstrating how simple changes in diet and lifestyle may cause substantial improvements in health and well-being, one of the most powerful interventions is the healing power of love and intimacy.

Power Strategies for a Lifetime

Living a balanced life, even under challenging conditions, is within reach and does not conflict with workplace success. Quite to the contrary, a plan that balances love and work is the decision of a lifetime and it will bring the biggest return on investment for executives and their families.

Bear in mind, The Ten Power Strategies are not merely random thoughts about what works in marital relationships. They were developed from listening to execs and their spouses and filtering what they had to say through three decades of working with and writing about couples as well as supervising other psychologists in their work with couples.

As a result, I learned what makes marriages fail, what makes them succeed, and what can make marriages a source of great meaning. By observing marital partners' interactions, facial expressions, and how they talk about their relationship to each other and to other people, here are my top ten suggestions for how to keep your marriage strong:

- **Commit:** Do you want to view your partner lovingly or not? Are you for your partner or against your partner? These may sound like strange questions, but many people in relationships are literally enemies. They put a negative spin on each other, just as enemies do. If you decide you want to love your partner, you can view him or her lovingly. You can choose to do things that make you feel good about each other, instead of acting in a manner that makes you feel bad. What brings you to behave in a way that brings you pain when it is just as easy to give love? That's an important question to ask yourself.
- **Deliver effectively:** You have a choice every time you say something to your partner. You can say something that will either nurture the relationship or tear it down. Arguments start when a spouse escalates the conflict by making a critical or contemptuous remark in a confrontational tone and gets a defensive response. In contrast, couples who avoid saying every angry thought when discussing touchy topics are consistently the happiest. It is best to state your concern using "I" statements rather than the more provocative and blame casting "you" statements. When you're feeling overwhelmed, make a deliberate effort to calm yourself before speaking. A respectful delivery is less likely to set you and your partner into the escalation cycle.
- **Foster collaboration:** In a happy marriage, couples make at least three times as many positive statements to and about each other and their relationship ("We laugh a lot") as opposed to negative ones ("We never have fun"). A marriage succeeds to the extent that both husband and wife can accept influence from each other. If a woman says, "Do you have to work Thursday night? Jimmy has a parent conference and I would like you to be there," and her husband replies, "My plans are set, and I'm not changing them," this guy is in a shaky marriage. The same applies to a woman

who is not mutually accommodating. However, this is less a concern of mine. A husband's ability to be persuaded by his wife (rather than vice-versa) is so crucial because, research shows, women are already well practiced at accepting influence from men, and a true partnership only occurs when a husband is able to do so as well. In short, a good marriage must have a rich climate of collaboration. Do not rely on New Year's resolutions. Apply the Mutual Support program to insure that you make deposits to your emotional bank account.

- **Create trust:** Trust is at the foundation of any relationship. The need to trust and be trusted continues throughout the life cycle. At every developmental level, we are more likely to have good relationships and succeed in whatever we do when our relationships are based on trust. In contrast, whenever trust breaks down, as psychologists well know, individual development is inhibited. We can't grow as fully as individuals, and we are less able, even *un*able, to have satisfying love relationships.
- **Speak from the heart:** In love relationships, feelings are the voice of the heart. Appealing to your partner's emotions often works more effectively than rational discourse. A love relationship does not center on sharing the rent or household chores or even co-parenting; it is distinguished by emotional involvement. So much of what really matters in love depends upon our feelings. When you tell your partner what you are feeling, that is a true experience by definition. No one can argue with you; only you know how you feel. Thoughts like, "I think you're a jerk" can be argued. If you feel judged, express it so that you can elicit and probe for what your partner is actually feeling. Letting your spouse know that you understand him or her is one of the most powerful tools for healing your relationship. It is an antidote to criticism, contempt, and defensiveness. Instead of attacking or ignoring your partner's point of view, you try to see the problem from his or her perspective and show that you think his or her viewpoint may have some validity.
- **Argue well:** Every relationship experiences conflict but not every couple has the skills to resolve it. Some couples respond to conflict by withdrawing emotionally; others respond by attacking the other spouse and failing to listen to their partner´s point of view. When a couple does not reduce conflict, they become vulnerable to divorce. Successful repair attempts include: owning your part in a conflict; using humor; stroking your partner with a caring remark ("I understand that this is hard for

you"); making it clear you're on common ground ("This is our problem"); backing down (in marriage, as in the martial art Aikido, it sometimes pays to yield); and, in general, being skillful and receptive to compromise as well as offering signs of appreciation for your partner along the way ("I really appreciate and want to thank you for . . ."). If an argument gets too heated, take a break, and agree to approach the topic again when you are both calm.

- **Provide models:** While some couples get mired in repetitive fights to which their children bear witness and others may even stop talking, other couples are even more ambitious combatants, they draw their children into their differences and form a triangle. Parents who create this triangle are playing out their personal or marital issues through their children. Successful couples do not draw their children into adult issues as referees, judges, targets or in any other biased role.
- **Assess regularly:** Awareness is the first step in healing, both individually and relationally. The value of behavioral science is to increase the level of awareness with which we face each day. This matters, not just a little, but a lot, and not just to the quality of our relational life but also to our survival. Feedback is central to awareness and to maintaining gains. Knowing how we are doing keeps us on track. If done properly, it is an early warning system that can help stem negative patterns—especially in the face of the stiff challenges to the exec marriage—and simultaneously serves as a confidence builder when we are doing well. Optimizing feedback requires the use of empathy, self-awareness and sensitivity. You've got to celebrate the strengths you and your partner have, as well as being realistic about limitations. Too often the focus is on deficiencies; this can be demoralizing rather than motivating.
- **Prevent relapse:** Relational competence cannot be improved overnight. Recall, the emotional brain learns new patterns over weeks and months, not days. We all learn a new skill more effectively if we have repeated chances to practice it over an extended period of time. Research indicates that actual practice has double the impact on job performance as the presentation of concepts alone. And the return on investment for practice during training is seven times greater than for the didactic sessions. This is a critical finding that applies equally to relationship competence. Over-learning, that is, practicing a new habit far beyond the point where you can do it well, greatly reduces the likelihood that you will

revert to the old habit under pressure. In that regard, the emotional conference is the most powerful strategy I have ever experienced for practicing several emotional skills within a fifteen-minute time period.

- **Seek help early:** Just as good feelings are based on positive behaviors from your partner and can lead to satisfaction, bad or hostile feelings that threaten marital happiness are created when the partner engages in a high frequency of negative behaviors. Early intervention is less painful and more effective than intervention in a relationship that has been worn down over a long period. Take action. A pattern of negative behavior raises a red flag. Seek help! The average couple waits six years before seeking help for marital problems (and keep in mind, half of all marriages that end do so in the first seven years). This means the average couple lives with unhappiness for far too long.

Intensive Care Tips

If after completing the ten strategies major problems remain unchanged, intensive care is indicated. One or both partners may suspect or fear that the relationship is bankrupt or irretrievably damaged as a result of chronic hostility. This may in fact be the case. There comes a time in some neglected relationships when the memory of joy is so distant and the possibility of its revival so improbable that parting appears more reasonable than interminable pain and loneliness.

In other instances, as with an individual attempting to survive a life-threatening illness, vital signs may be weak but their very existence is a signal of hope. For those who are discouraged but not yet hopeless, some intensive-care tips follow:

1. Whenever relationship distress is severe, a couple should reduce the number and complexity of tasks confronting them by notifying those around them, including their children, to temporarily make fewer demands. As much as possible, work-related projects and extra responsibilities (e.g., volunteer activities), which add to a hectic, pressured schedule, should be postponed for the time being. In a sense, an ailing relationship, like an ailing body, requires special attention and energy until it is strengthened.
2. Carefully consider the possible influence of external circumstances that may previously have been overlooked, such as failing health, career setbacks, and life transitions (for example, the last child going off to school

and leaving a housewife suddenly alone; or a midlife crisis typified by a concern about aging without having realized one's dreams). A close relationship should address itself to these issues, and avoidance will only add to the confusion.
3. Ask yourself, your trusted co-workers, and friends if your standards are unrealistic. You may be setting yourself up for disappointment by expecting perfect competence, generosity, and reliability from your partner.
4. Consider remaining in the relationship on a week-by-week basis. Long-range plans are too overwhelming when discouragement is running high. Think about a relationship-improvement goal for this week (or day). Building one slightly improved week or day upon another can eventually lead to a renewed relationship. By narrowing the focus to a manageable time span, the pressure either to make a lifelong commitment or to separate is reduced.
5. When distressed it is helpful for couples to make an active effort to move away from isolated couple interaction and toward an extended circle of family and friends. This often affords a better perspective and provides a potential background for understanding and breaking destructive, habitual patterns of relating.
6. One of the most common characteristics of a distressed relationship is an almost complete lack of humor. Every gesture, every movement, every word, is taken with deadly seriousness. Levity can sometimes be a powerful antidote to chronic bitterness. One couple, for example, has been fighting on an almost daily basis for many years about anything and everything. The pattern usually takes the form of one partner saying something to which the other has to respond one better.

She: You're just like your mother.
He: Better than being a stumbling drunk like your mother.

With humor, the same scene might go like this:

She: You're just like your mother.
He: *(starts mimicking his mother's facial expressions and gestures)*

In another instance, a woman becomes highly upset because her husband tells her she is brain dead each time he becomes frustrated. With humor in mind, I suggested to the wife that the next time her husband pronounces her brain dead, she should respond by calling an undertaker to make burial plans. Simply by taking this action she was able to maintain her composure and, at the same time, highlight the silliness of her partner's put-down. Certainly, not every provocation need be met with levity, but a sprinkling of laughter here and there can do wonders.

7. Give some thought to approaching a stalemate from a fresh perspective. A head-on confrontation, regardless of how skillfully it is worded, may not always work. An example from history reported by Paul Watzlawick and his associates in *Change*: During one of the many nineteenth-century riots in Paris, the commander of an artillery unit received orders to clear the city square and to fire on the assemblage if the people refused to disperse. Knowing that a warning to disassemble would only anger the crowd and lead to many deaths, the commander *reframed* the order, changed its meaning, so that it would be received peacefully. While his soldiers leveled their cannons at the square and silence fell on the crowd, the commander drew his sword and shouted for all to hear, "Mesdames, Messieurs, I have orders to fire at the *canaille* [disreputable persons, riff-raff], but as I see a great number of honest, respectable citizens before me, I request that they leave so that they are not mistakenly harmed." The square was emptied almost immediately.

Similarly, an imaginative individual in tune with his partner, can reframe a chronic relationship quarrel. One couple, for instance was fighting endlessly about the wife's overprotectiveness of their only son. The more her husband accused her of smothering their son, the more insecure she felt and the more restrictive she became. This pattern continued with great psychological cost to all involved until one day her husband approached her differently.

"You know dear," he began, "you really are a superbly concerned and competent parent. And I'm sure, for our son's sake, for his sense of independence and self-confidence, you would be willing to make the ultimate parental sacrifice by allowing him more freedom." When his comments were put this way—"for our son's sake," "parental sacrifice"—the wife no longer felt her competence was being threatened; she was now motivated to do something for her son, a challenge she couldn't resist.

Do not expect the suggestions above to be easily or quickly implemented. The greatest trap is to expect too much change too rapidly and too consistently. Further, particularly during this critical period, if you restrict your emotional existence exclusively to your relationship, you will, in all probability, intensify your feelings of being cheated and prematurely give up the struggle. A wiser approach is to fortify yourself on the nourishment that friends and individual interests provide as you navigate these difficult times.

New Beginnings

Our journey through the skills and principles of intimate relating began on a sad note. Recall, only a minority of men and women in the competitive and demanding executive boardroom are able to maintain a vibrant and fulfilling marriage. Yet most of us persevere in our struggle.

More execs are marrying and cohabiting now than ever before; even the perpetually escalating divorce rate does not act as a discouragement. Some of us may be disaffected with our partner, but we are still drawn to the concept of long-term commitment. In this regard, let's conclude with a more positive view of what this relationship can become.

Kenneth is a highly respected, award-winning photographer and the father of three children. He is a man who is occasionally exasperated by his wife but most often delighted and pleased by her company. "She is," he stated at the outset of our conversation, "my very best friend."

> I first met Nancy one summer weekend on the beach. It was an overcast day and the beach was nearly empty. I was just about to return home when I spotted this tall, good-looking redhead sitting alone. When I approached her she looked up matter-of-factly from her book, *From Good to Great*, and wasn't particularly friendly. But I was gently persistent. She told me, finally, that she was completing her MBA at Duke. I was pretty impressed; she really had exciting, ambitious goals. Finding a guy and getting married wasn't a top priority as it was with lots of women I encountered. What struck me about her was that she was so alive, so interesting. After we had relaxed a bit, we seemed to have so much to talk about. This wasn't just a beautiful woman; there was a real person under that pretty skin.
>
> We continued to see each other, and the following year Nancy graduated and accepted a very prestigious position with a Fortune 100 company. For the first couple of months I commuted to Boston and we spent our weekends together. After a while, though, we realized

how much we missed each other's company during the week. I moved my stuff up to Boston; as a pretty well-established freelancer, moving was no problem, and we found a little place. I'd come home after a day's work, we'd go out for a quick dinner, and then we'd return home, where she would be online doing research for her job until late at night. It was a grind, but I really loved seeing her progress—she has such a fine mix of the organizational, philosophic, and artistic minds. I felt about her as I had never felt about anyone. I was proud to know her.

We were married that fall, and over the next eight years, our three daughters—Jennifer, Katharine, and Alyson—were born. Nancy is still enormously involved in the business world. She also has a university faculty position, she is active in professional organizations, and she is a frequent contributor to the business literature. I, as usual, am passionately devoted to my work. Our life is busy, hectic, frequently bordering on the chaotic. I guess it's always been this way, even before the children. There have been periods when for days at a time, we'd meet each other only in bed. And nowadays, with the kids, especially if someone gets sick, the confusion at times is barely tolerable. I know Nancy is concerned about the impact of her frequent absence on the children; I often worry about my time with them also. When I really stop to think about it, they're getting along beautifully. They are thriving psychologically.

There are times when I think it would be much simpler, easier, more harmonious if Nancy didn't work, if she were more of a housewife. I think of my parents—my father worked and my mother catered to him. Life revolved around him. Honestly, sometimes when I'm dealing with the girls and I'm hungry and tired, I wish my wife were a bit more domestic. But then Nancy and I go out together, and I see other couples looking bored with each other, hardly ever making eye contact, not having anything to say to each other. That's when I reaffirm what we've developed. We're still courting each other after sixteen years. We always find each other interesting, stimulating. When Nancy talks about her work, her excitement is infectious. I don't know if I would be as pleased if I wasn't pretty successful in my own field, but I am. She has great respect for my work, and that means a lot to me. All in all, even though life with us is never simple, and sometimes things can even be very rough, there is no one I'd rather spend an evening with than Nancy.

No doubt, the way of life described above is busy and complicated; it calls for the scheduling talents of a network executive, the flexibility of a labor-relations negotiator, and the energy of a politician campaigning for re-election. Yet, although it may not be every couple's solution, it does provide this man and woman the mutual growth necessary for love.

And this is the task before each couple: to discover for themselves workable ways to keep their love alive. Loving without reservation, letting another person—someone who you have to face the next day and everyday—really get to know you, takes a degree of faith, self-awareness, and perhaps more than anything, courage. It is the courage to believe in yourself enough to be revealing and to tolerate the intensity of the experience.

It requires that you accept yourself, your humanness, including shortcomings; that with your imperfections you are still worthwhile. You have to take responsibility for your feelings and regard yourself enough to express them. It is a refusal to tolerate your own self-deceptions and to face your deepest truths. Doing this with your love partner is like walking a razor's edge. It is not for the faint of heart and it doesn't make life easier or painless. It just makes life sweeter and the pain more meaningful.

Discussion Forum

This experience will give you a chance to see the strengths of your marriage by comparing yourselves to other couples in your lives.

1. Each of you jot down the names of two different couples you both know. One should be an example of the worst marriage you know of, the other of the best marriage.

2. Now share the names with one another and tell why you feel the best marriage works and the worst marriage doesn't. Perhaps you admire how one couple expresses affection, or you disapprove of the way another couple berates one another.

3. Talk about your own marriage in relation to these well above average and well below average marriages. Compare the way you and your spouse manage to get through difficult times with the way each of these couples handle their challenges. Can you identify behaviors you want to avoid? Are there things you'd like to emulate?

4. Talk about your own ability as a couple to overcome obstacles. Have you weathered changes or incidents of which you're particularly proud? If so, what contributed to your success?

Mutual respect will catapult my marriage!

Afterword: Memo to the CEO

Your company is hemorrhaging money—and there are cost-effective solutions that are being neglected! Troubled marriages and those that end in divorce cost billions in lost productivity. "When people are going through difficult personal problems their work is no longer their priority," John Challenger, chief executive of the national outplacement firm, Challenger, Gray & Christmas, Inc. contends. He's not wrong; in fact he's stating the obvious.

A sampling of the research:

- Based on average earnings, in a national sample of men, work loss associated with marital problems translates into approximately $6.8 billion per year.
- The Ohio Psychological Association conducted a survey of executives of small businesses and found a link between troubled marriages and work loss. The majority of the executives reported that divorce had a very negative impact on workplace productivity.
- The findings of Drs. Scott Stanley and Howard Markman at the University of Denver conclude, "Marital intervention targeted at the 20 percent with the most marital distress would increase productivity."
- A study of senior executives' career paths found that one of the major factors in derailment or failure is a life in which work dominates everything else. Executives whose demanding work results in family distress was found to directly affect the internal functioning and economic success of an organization, not just the personal lives of individuals.

Again, this is a mere sample of the voluminous evidence pointing to the association between marital distress and the consequent loss of productivity.

The impact of work stress on marriage is inarguable. Yet businesses are failing in their efforts to execute solutions. For years now, companies have paid lip service to family-friendly policies. Bear in mind that achieving balance between home and life is a leading concern of employees, and those who achieve this work-life balance become the most motivated and productive workers.

Here are some proposals drawn from interviews with nearly one hundred executives and their spouses:

- Market strong marriages from within by expanding Employee Assistance Programs so that they offer marital counseling services.
- Partner with programs to reach your employees through marriage enrichment programs and other services that support marriage.
- Implement intervention programs that educate couples on various skills for preventing marital distress and enhancing their relationships. (Note: Research suggests that marital intervention programs could recoup productivity that was lost, a benefit that far outweighs the costs of implementing such a program.)
- Install marriage-friendly travel policies. For instance, permit executives who are on the road more than one-third of the time to have their spouses accompany them on selected business trips.
- Provide psychological support for families who are relocating. A dark secret among relocation consultants is that job transfers routinely strain marriages and sometimes trigger divorce.
- Create more liberal parenting leave by allowing parents to patch together as much paid time off as possible, including vacation, sick days and perhaps even a short-term disability policy. (*Note:* A study of working mothers suggests that mothers who take at least three months off after childbirth show significantly fewer symptoms of depression after they return to work, compared with women who take six weeks or less.)
- Initiate personnel policies and work environments that permit parents to spend more time with their children, thus helping to reduce the marital stress that accompanies childrearing. Examples include: opportunities for job sharing, compressed work weeks, career breaks, and working at home.

Return on Investment

As Allen Bergerson, director of personnel policy development at Eastman Kodak, notes: "In 1987, when our work-family task force proposed implementation of our family-supportive policies, management asked what rate of return could be expected on the investment. I responded that the savings or return could not be substantiated, but that the problems we were attempting to solve were costing more than the proposed investment, and that we were more than confident that the return would exceed the costs of the programs. Nothing has occurred since to shake that confidence."

As your reliance on women in the workforce has grown, it is imperative that you pay special attention to the 72 percent of mothers in the workforce with children under eighteen—they don't want to have to choose between a life that is 24/7 business and 24/7 domesticity. Many of the best are dropping out of high-pressure jobs rather than kill themselves trying to do it all.

Work/life balance is a cost-effective strategy that's totally consistent with business goals and will draw the best and most forward-looking executives to your organization. Choose talent on family-centered terms, rather than no talent or talent that will not stay committed.

Bibliography

Ali, Lorraine, and Miller, Lisa. "The New Infidelity: From Office Affairs to Internet Hookups." *Newsweek,* July 12, 2004.

Askt, Daniel. "On the Contrary; White-Collar Stress? Stop the Whining." *New York Times,* September 19, 2004.

Bergerson, Allen. The Conference Board, "Linking Work-Family Issues to the Bottom Line," Report 962 (1991), p. 11.

Donnelly, D. "Sexually Inactive Marriages." *Journal of Sex Research,* 30 (1993), 171–79.

Ellis, Albert. *Reason and Emotion in Psychotherapy.* New York: Lyle Stuart, 1962.

Fast, Julius, and Fast, Barbara. *Talking Between the Lines.* New York: Viking Press, 1979.

Flynn, Gillian. "Corporate Fallout from Failed Marriages." *Workforce Management,* March 2003, 64.

Gardner, Howard. *Frames of Mind.* New York: Basic Books, 1993.

Gergen, Kenneth J., Gergen, Mary M., and Barton, William H. "Deviance in the Dark." *Psychology Today,* October 1973, 129–30.

Goleman, Daniel. *Working with Emotional Intelligence.* New York: Bantam, 1998.

Harlow, Harry F. "The Nature of Love." *American Psychologist,* 13 (1958), 673-85.

——— and Harlow, M. "Learning to Love." *American Scientist,* 54, no. 3 (1966), 190–201.

Hollender, M. H. "Women's Wish to be Held: Sexual and Non-Sexual Aspects." *Medical Aspects of Human Sexuality,* October 1971, 12–26.

Kaslow, Florence W. (ed.). *Handbook of Relational Diagnosis and Dysfunctional*

Family Patterns (Wiley Series in Couples and Family Dynamics and Treatment) New Jersey: Wiley-Interscience, 1996.

Kazan, Elia. *The Arrangement*. New York: Scarborough House, 1967.

Koch, Joanne, and Koch, Lew. *The Marriage Savers*. New York: Coward, McCann & Geoghegan, 1976.

Lederer, William J., and Jackson, Don D. *The Mirages of Marriage,* New York: W. W. Norton, 1968.

Ligos, Melinda. "Business People; Memo to Spouse: I Really Do Care." *New York Times*, January 4, 2004.

Markman, H., Stanley, S., and Blumberg, S. *Fighting for Your Marriage* (revised and updated edition). San Francisco: Jossey Bass, 2001.

Montagu, Ashley. *Touching: The Human Significance of the Skin*. New York: Columbia University Press, 1971.

Parnes, Francine, "Business Travel; How Not to Spend Your Next, or First Honeymoon." *New York Times*, June 15, 2004.

Schwartz, John. "Always on the Job, Employees Pay with Health." *New York Times*, September 5, 2004.

Seligman, M.E.P., and Peterson, C. *Learned Helplessness*. In N. Smelser and P. Baltes (eds.). *International Encyclopedia for the Social and Behavioral Sciences* (vol. 13, p. 8583–86). New York: Elsevier, 2002.

Spencer, Lyle, M. Presentation to the International Personnel Management Association. Boston, June 1996.

Spencer, Lyle M., and Spencer, Signe. *Competence in Work, Models for Superior Performance*. New York: John Wiley and Sons, 1993.

Stratford, Sherman. "Leaders Learn to Heed the Voice Within." *Fortune*, August 22, 1994.

Vaihinger, Hans. *The Philosophy of As-If.* Translated by C. K. Ogden. New York: Charles Scribner's Sons, 1924.

Watzlawick, Paul, Weakland, John, and Fisch, Richard. *Change*. New York: W. W. Norton, 1974.

Index

ABC theory of personality, 40–42
Abdoo, Richard, 147–48
Academy of Management Journal, 100
Academy of Social Work, 176
Acceptance, Mutual Support program for, 63–67
Action plan, 185–93
  for conflict resolution, 119–26
Active collaboration, 48–53
Addictions, 78–80
Ad hoc teams. *See* Teams
Affairs (infidelity), 7, 19–23, 80–87
  tool kit for dealing with, 87–90
Affection, 22–23. *See also* Touch
Agee, William, 81
Agenda, for emotional conference, 149, 150
All-or-nothing behavior, 124
American Association of Marriage and Family Therapy, 176
American Board of Professional Psychologists (ABPP), 175
American Board of Psychiatry, 174
American Psychological Association (APA), 170
Anatomy, of failing relationship, 15–18
Apologies, 87–88
Appointment, 124–25
  for emotional conference, 147, 149

Arguments (arguing), 171, 187, 188–89
Arrangement, The (Kazan), 110–11
Arrow Electronics, 1–2
Assessment. *See also* Feedback
  of therapists, 178–80
Attentive listening, 151
Attitude, 26–28, 38–40, 46, 117
Avoidance, of partner, 171
"Awfulizing," 158

"Bad Parent" game, 133–34
Bargaining, 119–26
  tool kit for, 126–28
Bendix Corporation, 81
Bergerson, Allen, 199
"Better Parent" game, 133
Bibliography, 201–2
Blame (blaming), 32–34, 37–40, 45, 151
Blank, Don, 84
Blind spots, 95–97
Body contact, 58–62
Body language, 100–103, 107
Boredom, at home, 37
Breaches, 74–77. *See also* Affairs
Buffering, 137–38
Business trips, 53–56, 103–4, 198

Care (caring), 48–58
  active, 48–53

INDEX

Care (caring) (*cont.*)
  long-distance, 53–56
  tool kit for, 62–67
Carnavale, Anthony, 97–98
Center for Creative Leadership, 8, 74, 130
Challenger, John, 197
Change, 34–37
  fear of, 42–45
  tool kit for, 45–46
Change (Watzlawick), 105–6, 192
Checkups. *See* Feedback
Children (Strategy Seven), 2–3, 130–44, 189
  communication with, 92–93
  defensive games and, 137–39
  discussion forum, 144
  fighting and, 132–37, 139–43
  stay at home dads, 6–7, 35–37
  team building and, 130–32
  tool kit for, 143–44
  triangulation and, 132–37, 189
Closed-door policy, 92
Cognitive-behavior therapy, 40–41
Collaboration (Strategy Three), 48–67, 187–88
  active caring, 48–53
  discussion forum, 67
  long-distance caring, 53–56
  role of touch, 58–62
  romance and, 56–58
  tool kit, 62–67
Commitment (Strategy One), 15–31, 187
  anatomy of failing relationship, 15–18
  challenges to, 20–24
  discussion forum, 31
  expectations and, 26–28
  relationship-enhancement inventory for, 24–26
  taking a stand, 28–31
  tipping point, 19–20
  tool kit, 30–31
Communication. *See also* Skillful communication
  definition of, 91–92
  relationship-enhancement inventory and, 24, 25–26
Competence in Work, Models for Superior Performance (Spencer), 130, 147
Compromise (compromising), 119–26
  tool kit for, 126–28
Conference. *See* Emotional conference
Confessions, 84–87
Confidant, treating child as, 143
Conflict resolution (Strategy Six), 110–29, 188–89
  action plan for, 119–26
  discussion forum, 129
  fighting and, 112–19
  relationship-enhancement inventory and, 24, 25–26
  tool kit for, 126–28
  vision and, 110–12
Connectedness, 149
Conventional thinking, 36–37
Cornell University, 18
Cortisone, 3
Couples therapy. *See* Therapy
Creating lasting value. *See* Lasting value
Creative Visions Consulting, 2–3
Credibility, and infidelity, 74, 75
Cunningham, Mary, 81
Current market conditions, 15–67

Danger signals, 171, 181
Defensiveness, 118
Delivery, 102–3, 187
Demands, versus expressing feelings, 45

Denial, 84
Developmental Psychology, 140–41
DINS (Double Income, No Sex), 6, 19, 48–50, 57–58
Discussion forums, 196
 children, 144
 collaboration, 67
 commitment, 31
 conflict resolution, 129
 emotional conference, 159
 feedback, 166
 skillful communication, 109
Disguised requests, 106–7, 108–9
Disillusionment, 15–16, 72–74
Distractions, 30
Donnelly, Denise, 23
Donnelly Corporation, 160–61
Double Income, No Sex (DINS), 6, 19, 48–50, 57–58
Duration of therapy, 180–81

Eastman Kodak, 199
Educational system, 5–8
Ellis, Albert, 40–42
E-mail, keeping in touch with, 54
Emotional conference (Strategy Eight), 147–59, 189–90
 benefits of, 150–57
 discussion forum, 159
 essential competencies, 147–49
 guidelines for, 149–50
 self-soothing and, 157–59
Emotional intelligence, 10–11
Emotions (feelings), 45, 107–8, 125
 expressing your, 92–95, 151, 188
Empathic listening (empathy), 97–100, 109
Empowerment, 37–40, 158
Empty-nest adjustment, 161–62
Epictetus, 40
Exchange attitude, 120–26

Excuses, making, 28–31
Executive marriages, overview of, 1–11
Expectations, power of, 26–28
Extended families, 131
Extramarital affairs. *See* Affairs
Eye contact, 101, 102

Facial expressions, 100–103, 107
Fairness, in negotiations, 122
Family issues, in emotional conferences, 152–56, 158–59
Family-promoting decisions, 49–50
Family teamwork. *See* Children
Family time, 49, 54–55
Fault lines, 74–77
Fear (fear-of-change principle), 42–45
Feedback (Strategy Nine), 160–66, 189
 discussion forum, 166
 inventory, 164–65
 measuring performance, 160–62
 preparation for, 162–63
Feelings (emotions), 45, 107–8, 125
 expressing your, 92–95, 151, 188
Fees, for therapy, 180–81
Fights (fighting), 112–19, 152–53
 with children, 132–37, 139–43
 emotional conferences, 152–56
Financial setbacks, 17, 18
Flexibility, in negotiations, 122
Florida Couple and Family Institute, 111
Forgiveness, 159, 166
Frames of Mind (Gardner), 167–68
Freud, Sigmund, 181

Gambler's Anonymous, 79–80
Gambling, 79–80
Games, and triangulation, 132–39
Gardner, Howard, *Frames of Mind,* 167–68

INDEX

Gender roles, 61, 113–14, 128. *See also* SAHD
Generalities, 103–7, 108–9
Gergen, Kenneth, 59
Goals, 28–31, 191
Golden Rule, 57–58
Goleman, Daniel, *Working with Emotional Intelligence,* 62–63, 147–48, 160–61
Gottman, John, 140–41
Gradual approach, to change, 45–46
Gripe sessions, 147–48

Harlow, Harry F., 59–60
Have-it-all notion, 36
Health issues, 4, 8, 180–81
Henley, Edward, 43–44
Hollender, Marc H., 60–61
Hugs (hugging), 61
Humor, 191–92

I Don't Know How She Does It (Pearson), 3
Indirectness, 103–7, 108–9
Individual Responsibility, 37–40
Infidelity (affairs), 7, 19–23, 80–87
  tool kit for dealing with, 87–90
Inner voice, 30–31
Integrity, 74, 75
Intensive-care tips, 190–93
International Negotiation, 121
Interruptions, 128, 147, 150
Inventory
  feedback, 162–65
  relationship-enhancement, 24–26
Investment, protection of. *See* Emotional conference
"I" statements, 45, 125, 149–50, 156–57, 187
Jackson, Don, *The Mirages of Marriage,* 38–39

Jenkins, Jim, 2–3
Jennings, Kate, *Moral Hazards,* 3
Journal of Marriage and the Family, 2
Journal of Sex Research, 23
Journals (journal writing), 54
"Just do it," 23

Kahn, William, 100
Kaslow, Florence, 111
Katz, Lynn Fainsilber, 140–41
Kazan, Elia, *The Arrangement,* 110–11
Kelman, Herbert, 121
Koch, Joanne and Lew, *The Marriage Savers,* 137

Labor, U. S. Department of, 97–98, 151
Lasting value (Strategy Four), 71–90, 188
  discussion forum, 90
  extramarital affairs, 80–87
  fault lines, 74–77
  great divide, 77–80
  quiet virtues, 71–74
  tool kit for, 87–90
Laughter, 191–92
Lederer, William, *The Mirages of Marriage,* 38–39
Length of therapy, 180–81
Letters, keeping in touch with, 54
Lies (lying), 74–77
Listening, 30, 128, 151
  tuning in, 97–100
Long-distance caring, 53–56
Long-term development plan, 147–81
Lovemaking (sex), 22–23, 60–61, 171. *See also* Romance; Touch

McCarthy, Patrick, 62–63
Marital therapists, 173, 176–77
Marital therapy. *See* Therapy
Marketing plan, 71–144

Markman, Howard, 111, 197
Marriage and Family Living, 95
Marriages, overview of executive, 1–11
Marriage Savers, The (Koch), 137
Medical Aspects of Human Sexuality, 60–61
Middle ground, in negotiations, 122–23
Mirages of Marriage, The (Lederer and Jackson), 38–39
Montagu, Ashley, *Touching*, 59
Mood and meaning, in communication, 91–95
Moral Hazards (Jennings), 3
Murdoch, Rupert and Anna, 5
Mutual exchange, 120–26
Mutual Support program, 63–67

Nasser, Jacques, 5
National Business Travel Monitor, 54–55
National Institutes of Health, 139
Navy, U. S., 27
Negative therapeutic reactions, 181
Negativity (negative statements), 45, 97, 104–5, 127–28, 187–88
Negotiations (negotiating), 119–26
  tool kit for, 126–28
Newlywed Game (TV show), 95
Newsweek, 7, 20, 91
New York Times, 1, 2, 4, 54–56
Nonverbal messages, 100–103, 107

Occupational Environmental Medicine, 3
Office affairs, 80–87
Ohio Psychological Association, 197
On-the-job coaching, 169–70. See also Therapy
Open requests, 106–7, 108–9
Over-dependence, 171
Over-learning, 189–90
Oxford English Dictionary, 59

Parenting. See Children
Parnes, Francine, 54–56
Patience, 126
Pearson, Allison, *I Don't Know How She Does It*, 3
Perceptions, 40–42
Persistence, 46, 144
Personal attitude, 26–28, 38–40, 46, 117
Personnel policies, at work, 198
Pessimism (pessimistic attitude), 26–27
Peterson, David, 170
Peterson, Donald, 62–63
Pharmaceutical therapy, 174, 175
Phone calls, keeping in touch with, 54
Physical affection, 22–23, 58–62
Politeness, 32, 51
"Poor Little Me" game, 136–37
Porcupines, 116
Positive attitude, 26–28, 46, 127–28
Positive reframing, 40–42, 192
Positive statements, 45, 97, 125, 187–88
Powerless attitude, 38–40
Power of expectation, 26–28
Power Strategies Action Plan, 185–93. See also entries beginning with "Strategy"
Practice (practicing), 189–90. See also Emotional conference
Progress report. See Feedback
Psychiatrists, 173, 174
Psychologists, 173, 175
Psychotherapy, 174

Quiet virtues, 71–74
RCA, 51
Reader's Digest, 77
Recommendations, for therapists, 177
Red flags, 171, 181
Redstone, Sumner and Phyllis, 5

INDEX

Reframing, 40–42, 192
Relapses, 189–90. *See also* Emotional conference
Relationship checkup. *See* Feedback
Relationship-enhancement inventory, 24–26
Requests, 106–7, 108–9, 125
Resources. *See* Therapy
Retirement, 162
Right-versus-wrong attitude, 117
Role playing, 67, 98–99, 126–27
Romance, 56–58. *See also* Touch
Romantic love, myth of, 95
Ruderman, Marian, 8

SAHD (Stay At Home Dads), 6–7, 35–37
Sales strategy, 71–144
Schedules (scheduling), 23, 190
 family time, 49
Secrets (secrecy), 77–80, 86–87
Self-awareness, 149, 150–51, 156–57, 189
Self-empowerment, 37–40, 158
Selfishness, 57–58
Self-soothing, 157–59
Seligman, Martin, 140
Sex. *See* Lovemaking
Sexual harassment, 80
Sexual infidelity. *See* Infidelity
Should-makers, 127
Single-parent families, 131
Skillful communication (Strategy Five), 91–108, 188–89
 blind spots and, 95–97
 definition of, 91–92
 discussion forum, 109
 getting to the point, 103–7
 mood and meaning, 91–95
 nonverbal messages, 100–103, 107
 tool kit for, 107–9
 tuning in, 97–100
Small talk, 93–94
Social workers, 173, 175–76
Soloman, Paul, 137
Sopranos, The (TV show), 20
Southern Methodist University, 151
Spencer, Lyle, 52–53, 130, 147
Spencer, Signe, 130
Stanley, Scott, 197
Stay At Home Dads (SAHD), 6–7, 35–37
Strategy One (success begins with commitment), 15–31, 187
 anatomy of failing relationship, 15–18
 challenges to, 20–24
 discussion forum, 31
 expectations and, 26–28
 relationship-enhancement inventory for, 24–26
 taking a stand, 28–31
 tipping point, 19–20
 tool kit, 30–31
Strategy Two (unity, not division), 32–47, 187
 blame game and, 32–34
 change and, 34–37
 discussion forum, 47
 empowering yourself, 37–40
 overcoming fear, 42–45
 positive reframing, 40–42
 tool kit for, 45–46
Strategy Three (developing culture of collaboration), 48–67, 187–88
 active caring, 48–53
 discussion forum, 67
 long-distance caring, 53–56
 role of touch, 58–62
 romance and, 56–58
 tool kit, 62–67

Index

Strategy Four (creating lasting value), 71–90, 188
  discussion forum, 90
  extramarital affairs, 80–87
  fault lines, 74–77
  great divide, 77–80
  quiet virtues, 71–74
  tool kit for, 87–90
Strategy Five (skillful communication), 91–108, 188–89
  blind spots and, 95–97
  definition of, 91–92
  discussion forum, 109
  getting to the point, 103–7
  mood and meaning, 91–95
  nonverbal messages, 100–103, 107
  tool kit for, 107–9
  tuning in, 97–100
Strategy Six (building on strengths), 110–29, 188–89
  action plan for, 119–26
  discussion forum, 129
  fighting and, 112–19
  relationship-enhancement inventory and, 24, 25–26
  tool kit for, 126–28
  vision and, 110–12
Strategy Seven (growing children effectively), 130–44, 189
  communication with, 92–93
  defensive games and, 137–39
  discussion forum, 144
  fighting and, 132–37, 139–43
  stay at home dads, 6–7, 35–37
  team building and, 130–32
  tool kit for, 143–44
  triangulation and, 132–37, 189
Strategy Eight (protecting investment), 147–59, 189–90
  benefits of, 150–57
  discussion forum, 159
  essential competencies, 147–49
  guidelines for, 149–50
  self-soothing and, 157–59
Strategy Nine (assessing progress), 160–66, 189
  discussion forum, 166
  inventory, 164–65
  measuring performance, 160–62
  preparation for, 162–63
Strategy Ten (maximizing resources), 167–81, 190
  assessment of, 178–80
  cost of, 180
  danger signals and, 171
  discussion forum, 181
  expectations of, 172–73
  length of, 180–81
  preliminary screening tips, 170
  search for, 177–78
  types of, 173–77
Strayer, Jacqueline, 1–2
Strengths, building. *See* Conflict resolution
Stress, 3, 48
Support program, 63–67
Support, relationship-enhancement inventory and, 24, 25–26
Supportive touch, 58–62
Swarthmore College, 59

Talking. *See* Communication; Skillful communication
Teams (team building), 130–32
Telephone calls, keeping in touch with, 54
Ten Power Strategies Action Plan, 185–93. *See also* entries beginning with "Strategy"

INDEX

Therapy (therapists) (Strategy Ten), 49, 167–81, 190
   assessment of, 178–80
   cost of, 180
   danger signals and, 171
   discussion forum, 181
   expectations of, 172–73
   length of, 180–81
   preliminary screening tips, 170
   search for, 177–78
   types of, 173–77
3M, 8
Time-outs, 50, 99, 147
Tipping point, 19–20
To-do lists, 24, 63–64
Tool kits, 185–86
   for affairs, 87–90
   for children, 143–44
   for collaboration, 62–67
   for commitment, 30–31
   for conflict resolution, 126–28
   for skillful communication, 107–9
   for unity, 45–46
Touch (touching), 58–62
Touching (Montagu), 59
Training, 177
   marital therapists, 176–77
   psychiatrists, 174
   psychologists, 175
   social workers, 175–76
Travel (business trips), 53–56, 103–4, 198
Triangulation, 132–37, 189
Trust (trustworthiness), 71–77, 89–90, 171, 188. *See also* Lasting value
Tuning in, 97–100

Two-income couples. *See* DINS
Type A behaviors, 33–34, 42–43

Unity (Strategy Two), 32–47, 187
   blame game and, 32–34
   change and, 34–37
   discussion forum, 47
   empowering yourself, 37–40
   overcoming fear, 42–45
   positive reframing, 40–42
   tool kit for, 45–46
University of Denver, 111, 197
University of Pennsylvania, 140

Validators, 99
Value. *See* Lasting value
Vanderbilt School of Medicine, 60–61
Van Horn, Carl E., 2
"Victim/Villain" game, 134–35
Vindictiveness, 104–5
Virtues, 71–74
Vision, 110–12
Visualization, 31
Voight, Kevin, 8

Wall Street Journal, 1–2
Watzlawick, Paul, *Change,* 105–6, 192
Welch, Jack and Jane, 5
Who's Afraid of Virginia Woolf (play), 140
Wisconsin Energy, 147–48
Workaholics (workaholism), 48–50
Working with Emotional Intelligence (Goleman), 62–63, 147–48, 160–61
Workplace Basics: The Skills Employers Want (Carnavale), 97–98

About the Author

DR. JOEL BLOCK is a clinical psychologist practicing couples therapy on Long Island, in New York, where he has been honored with the Marriage and Family Therapist of the Year award.

A diplomate of the American Board of Professional Psychology, Dr. Block is a senior psychologist on the staff of Long Island Jewish Medical Center and an assistant clinical professor at the Albert Einstein College of Medicine.

He is the author of numerous magazine articles and fourteen books including *Naked Intimacy: How to Increase True Openness in Your Relationship*, *Broken Promises, Mended Hearts: Maintaining Trust in Love Relationships*, *Sex Over 50*, and *Secrets of Better Sex*.

Dr. Block and his wife, Gail, give seminars for couples several times a year.

His website is drblock.com and he can also be reached at his e-mail address, drblock@couplerelationships.com.

Dr. Block has appeared on several national television shows and has done countless radio shows.